UNVEILING THE
POLITICAL
AGENDA
OF JESUS

The Complete Time-Tested Truth
That Will Set You Free from Oppressive Regimes,
Failing Political and Financial Systems, Religious Confusion,
One-World Government and Fake Prosperity Gospels

Dr. Henry Tabifor

FALSE TEACHER

Unveiling the Political Agenda of Jesus

Dr. Henry Tabifor

Email: henry@tabiforleadershipfoundation.com

Website: www.tabiforleadershipfoundation.com

ISBN: 978-1-7352949-0-2

Published in the United States of America

Editorial Note: We have chosen to violate some grammatical rules by not capitalizing certain names and pronouns except when quoted.

Scripture quotations are from the New King James Version, copyright 1979, 1980, 1982, and 1994 by Thomas Nelson Inc.

Dedication

This book is dedicated to the late Dr. Myles Munroe.

As a student of the kingdom school of thought and an ambassador of the kingdom of heaven, most of the reflections I have included in this book were inspired by the Spirit of truth and the teachings of the renowned educator, motivational speaker and visionary leader Dr. Munroe, who introduced me to the truth about myself, my purpose and my destiny.

Contents

Acknowledgments

A vision to a generation is never given to and accomplished by one person. I have been inspired and encouraged by people I have met and some I may never meet. I owe a debt of gratitude to a very dear daughter Nancy, who worked tirelessly to review the drafts and to my queen baby girl, Glory, who kept the title of the book reverberating in our household. My dear mother—Helen, and lovely wife—Miranda, deserve endless thanks for their love and support.

To the young generation of thinkers in the United States of America and Uganda (Joy Kish, Lionel Tabifor, Chizoba Madubuko, Victoria Ajayi, Nancy Kyohirwe, Faith Tabifor, Martha Kakooza) who deliberated on the initial concepts of this book and encouraged me to document truth that will become a legacy for the next generation and beyond. This book is for you, your peers, and children.

Thanks to Dr. Nicolas Otieno, who reviewed the initial draft and validated it as a "game changer." I also appreciate the encouragement received from Prof. P.L.O. Lumumba, whose kind words will not be forgotten. Thanks also to my friends and the leadership of the National Program for Peace in the Cameroon, whose agenda for peace in the nation inspired me to think about church and politics. To H.E. Ambassador Arikana Chihombori-Quao, whose political insight inspired and challenged my thinking regarding colonization and love for all humanity.

To these great men and women whose messages and books have been the anchor of my kingdom walk since 1994. Words cannot express my sincere gratitude. They include Adeline Kapella—the lady who held my hand into the kingdom, Pastors Barry Smith, Samuel Kanyaki, Don Martini, Fred Muna, Pat Robertson, Zac Fomum, Benny Hinn, Mensa Otabil, Paul Crouch, Rod Parsley, Joyce Meyer, Dayo Olutayo, Perry Stone, George Adegboye, Clearance McClendon, Daniel Chumbow, T.D. Jakes, Jim Wambua, Juanita Bynum, John Francis, Dumsani Dube, Creflo Dollar, Joel Osteen, David Oyedepo, Marcus Lamb, Joseph Prince, Chris Oyakhilome, John Hagee, Charles Stanley, Kish Ufot, Derek Prince, Victor Odundo, Ron Carpenter, Henry Okonofua, Stephen Chandler and Sunday Adelaja.

To my bosom friends Prof. David Irefin, Mr. Mike Bisi and Dr. Uche Chukwurah, whose love and care prepared me for my life's encounter. Not forgetting my Hebrew friend Dr. David Silverstein, who helped me to understand the Hebrew culture both at his home and the Synagogue.

I must also thank Charisa and Myles Jr. for outstandingly carrying out the legacy of Dr. Myles and Ruth Munroe. Your generation owe you a debt of gratitude.

Finally, to all my collaborators in the Father's business, colleagues in the medical profession and United Nations. Together, we are making history.

Endorsement

I hereby endorse this masterpiece of work as authentic and represents a new cutting-edge approach to the political agenda of Jesus Christ. I have known Dr. Henry Tabifor as a prolific thinker and writer. Apart from his profession as a medical doctor, he has inspired a new generation of young people seeking to know and embrace the truth of the establishment of the government of heaven on earth. It is my conviction that in these pages one will find the milestones of wisdom from the author's heart and mind.

Prof. P.L.O. Lumumba
Global Peace Activist,
Advocate of the High Courts of
Kenya and Tanzania,
Certified International Mediator.

Purpose

Unveiling the Political Agenda of Jesus is about a King who sent his Son, from his kingdom, into his colony to recapture power from an illegally established government and return the governing authority to the rightful heirs.

The book:

> ➤ Engages the question regarding the purpose of our existence, self-identity, origin, potential and destiny
> ➤ Provokes readers and leaders to re-examine their belief systems about creation and theories of evolution and thus decipher why kingdoms are fast disappearing and national governments failing
> ➤ Stirs up a healthy debate on whether Jesus was a politician or a religious figure, and whether he established a governing system or a religious organization
> ➤ Exposes the existence of religious confusion, as well as the emergence of a new humanism and one-world government
> ➤ Expounds and demystifies the concepts and the ramifications of colonization, declarations of independence, freedom, and self-governance

> ➢ Encourages champions of freedom to empower fol-
> lowers and implores leaders to groom and pass on the
> baton to the next generation
> ➢ Sends a clarion call to ambassadors of Christ to re-
> examine the message they are conveying to humanity

Finally, Unveiling the Political Agenda of Jesus explores answers to the question; Can the government from heaven fill
the yearning of mankind for a perfect government in the face
of failing states, religious confusion, and global anarchy?

Introduction

The Dilemma of Living in a Colony with Two Masters: A Clash of Cultures

G rowing up in a close community, some of my fondest memories are those of my grandparents telling stories and tales of great men and women, the spirit world, and creatures that walked and crept on the earth and those that hovered above the air and dwelled beneath the waters. The children in my community were given informal education that comprised of traditions and norms that were unexplained and passed down from one generation to the next.

When I finally enrolled in the colonial missionary school, storytelling was upgraded to a subject called history. We studied European and English history—how Britain colonized America, Australia, and Japan; how the French, English, Germans, Portuguese and Belgians divided and colonized Africa; how independence wars were fought and lost, and so on. It was exciting to learn about the world, colonization, slave trade and wars of independence, being that my country had obtained independence from the English rule a couple of years earlier. These lessons filled my mind with so many questions, and as much as I enjoyed them, there was a clash of cultures between the informal and formal education I was receiving.

Our religious study classes and devotions created even more confusion. Stories of the Jews, their God and his Son, Jesus—as savior of the world, born of a virgin in Bethlehem— did not add up. It was difficult to comprehend how God as king would allow his people, the Jews, to be enslaved, how a king would be born into a colonized territory and in a manger in- stead of a palace. To add to all the confusion, the fact that his birth had been prophesied about seven thousand years before he was born. Any attempts to question what was considered sacred and mysterious was blasphemy. It was courteous to just say amen and make the sign of the cross. Nothing was ever mentioned about our ancestral gods and altars that we could see and feel. It was quite frustrating to be torn between the co- lonial god and the ancestral gods.

Furthermore, the reason behind colonization and the lib- eration struggle for independence were hardly explained. The intent of the colonial masters to capture new territory, expand their culture, and secure resources was hardly men- tioned during our history lessons. It appeared the educational system was structured to teach historical and scientific facts without providing in-depth truth, the why or purpose behind such events.

Not to discredit all that I was taught, some explanations on forms of colonization were offered. For instance, the Roman Empire, instead of transporting captives back to Rome opted to leave the citizens in their native land and imposed the Roman culture on them. That explained why the people in my community were not being traded as slaves anymore—because the colonizers implemented the same strategy as the Romans when they sent governors or regents and constructed colonial schools, hospitals, roads, railways and residential areas in the colonies.

As an adult in my quest for truth, I wondered where traditions, colonization and religion converged with the gospel of the kingdom that Jesus preached. Several questions, some of which have been posed below, were mind-boggling to me:

- Is God, whom Jesus claimed sent him to bring a new governing system on earth, a colonial master?
- Of all the eras and civilizations that came and went, why did God choose a Roman colony for the birth of his Son?
- What did Jesus mean when he said, "The kingdom of heaven has returned?"
- When did the kingdom leave the earth, and how was he going to re-establish it?
- If God is all-knowing and powerful, why did he not stop the rebellion in the garden of Eden but chose the lengthy and painful route of sending his Son to be rejected and crucified as a ransom for disobedience?

3

- ➤ What makes God's political agenda and ideology of governance different from the world's view?
- ➤ What unique policies and governing systems does he possess to attack, defeat, and replace the current global governing systems?
- ➤ If Jesus possesses so much power, why did he not form an army to overthrow the then-existing world government systems or choose terrorism as a route to advance his ideology?
- ➤ Why did Jesus condemn violence and even rebuke his followers when they opted to stir up rebellion against authority?
- ➤ Was Jesus Christ a religious leader and his church a religious organization or a king of a kingdom government and his church a political assembly?
- ➤ If Jesus is a religious figure, why then did he not pick his disciples from among the religious leaders?
- ➤ Is colonization a human concept? If yes, then why are governments unable to address world issues today?
- ➤ Could it be that the concept of colonization was misconstrued by both the colonial masters and the subjects in the colony?
- ➤ Could this misunderstanding underpin the evolution of evil kings and failed kingdoms, lords and subjects, rich and poor nations, dysfunctional governments and democratic confusion, terrorism, and global anarchy?
- ➤ Is recolonization of the earth by a new governing system a viable alternative to the cry for a new world order and leadership to resolve the imminent global crisis?

Indeed, there remain more questions than answers to these issues. It is my understanding that no one person, no matter how smart, can travel this journey alone to unravel these mysteries. We should walk the journey together, reasoning with one another, not just on the what, where, and how, but most importantly, the why of things. Taking our bearings from history books that inform us of what happened where and how, and then examining them against the Word of God that tells us why these events occurred. It is also necessary for us to look at the lives of great kings and kingdoms, various aspects of colonization, cultural expansion, and other forms of governments. Where else would anyone choose to start this journey but at the very beginning, the genesis of creation vis-à-vis the theory of evolution and a creator.

PART I

THE KING, HIS KINGDOM, ROYAL FAMILY AND THE COLONY

Chapter 1

Creation, Evolution, and a Creator

*It takes more faith to believe in the evolution of the universe
than to believe in a creator.*

Over the centuries, philosophers, scientists, archaeolo-gists, cosmologists, geologists, historians and religious scholars have researched and debated on how the universe came into existence, how living things evolved from non-living ones, and, more importantly, on the origin of mankind. Amazingly, the debate rages on even in the 21st century, in the face of global innovations in information and technology.

The universe is a complex masterpiece of wonder and sometimes mysterious. The complexity becomes even harder to comprehend when one tries to figure out which came first—the planets or the world? The planets are the physical territories, while the world is the cosmos, influence or sys-tems operating on these territories. The governing systems on planet earth have shifted from primitive to civilized worlds, revolutions to independence, and tyrannies to democracies. We are yet to witness the end game.

How our universe originated is a million-dollar question. If indeed the universe evolved from nothing, then it would be the greatest miracle in history. To imagine that it was created becomes even more intriguing. Who then is that creator? What is his nature and intention for creating the planets and the systems that govern them?

The theories of evolution, often referred to as the laws of natural selection and creation, hang on the balance. One may be tempted to imagine that evolution and creation may just be two sides of the same coin. Nevertheless, something cannot evolve from nothing. Creation may not necessarily cancel evolution, but it could simply be a de facto process of creation.

The theory of a single cell dividing and transforming itself into diverse non-living and living things is startling. Science is yet to discover the origin of the single cell, unravel the paradox of its replicative intelligence, and demonstrate the genetic linkage between mankind and the proposition of the chimpanzee as our ancestor. Even if one day it does, it will still have to answer the question why over the years fish have not changed the way they swim, neither have birds changed the way they fly, but mankind in the 21st century has gone supersonic into the deepest oceans and highest skies.

Over the centuries most of those who researched and philosophized to give humanity an explanation to the origin of the universe—either through evolutionary or creative theories—passed into eternity even before their jobs were done. Hence no definite conclusion has been established regarding our origin, creation, and evolution of the universe. This is understandable because the journey to understanding creation, evolution and a creator begins and ends with every individual.

There is a "knowing" or a gut feeling deep within the human soul or subconscious mind that recognizes a higher being that created all things. This subconscious feeling, which cannot be easily explained, is part of our being and can be seen in our daily lives and in nature. The "knowing" evolves as we grow, learn, meditate, and do a soul search on various issues of life, including death.

It is a common practice to hear theologians say that those who seek the Creator will find him. This speaks volumes. It could be the crux of the matter that challenges us to look inward, rather than depending on the thoughts and writings of others who were and are still searching. If the Creator has the willingness to reveal himself to those who seek him, then one loses nothing by asking him to reveal himself to them. There is no doubt such a creator will reveal himself to avoid remaining an illusion and denying himself the honor he deserves.

Throughout history, great men, and women, including atheists, have testified that you can find the Creator of the universe when you seek him personally. But the craving must be deep and genuine. The great scholar and renowned speaker on issues of evolution, creation and purpose, the late Dr. Myles Munroe, had this to say in one of his writings: "God is omnipotent but reveals himself only to those who seek him genuinely. If you seek him, he will reveal himself to you, and if you do not, he will hide himself from you. Atheists can't find God even though his manifest glory is seen in all of nature, because they are not interested in finding God."[1] In essence, one can only find what they are looking for. If indeed one is searching for the truth about God, he will reveal himself and the purpose of his creation.

The truth keeps staring at us irrespective of race, gender, creed, and status as we attempt to answer questions of identity, origin, purpose, potential and destiny. How wonderful and fulfilling life would be if we had answers to all these questions. The emptiness and yearning for fulfillment in our lives would vanish like morning dew at sunrise.

Guess what! The Creator, whose handiwork is hidden behind the laws and theories of evolution has not hidden his divine plans and purpose for the universe from us. From time immemorial, his invisible attributes are clearly seen in nature and engraved in our hearts. Philosophy, cosmology, occultism, and religion have tried to fill the void in our hearts but failed.

The human soul is restless until it finds God. The Creator is known by revelation; he has revealed himself in every heart, but many suppress that truth and speak against his existence (Romans 1:18–25). Unbelievers are not fools, but people living in denial. It is commonly said, "Dying men speak the truth,"[2] and this has been the case with many who do not believe as they take their last breath on planet earth. Some have been heard whispering and confessing the existence of the Creator, whom they ignored throughout their life experiences. Others have had a "come-to-Jesus- moment"[3] because they finally found themselves unable to keep up with the tides.

Anyone who catches the revelation of the Creator never ceases to wonder how great he is. It is an indescribable feeling that causes one to start seeing his wonderful works engraved in all of creation. It is a "re-birth" that awakens and reintroduces you to yourself and answers the questions of origin and identity: Who and whose you are?

Confusion sets in when one tries to understand the Creator through the eyes of others who are quite often more confused and helpless. It is a fulfilling experience when one personally reasons with and seeks the Creator to reveal himself. Many who have ventured on such personal trips into the heart of the Creator have lived to tell the story. Songs like "Blessed Assurance"[4] and "Amazing Grace"[5] were written by great men and women who thought they had and knew it all, only to discover greater peace in their souls when they found the Creator of the universe and yielded to his authority.

When you return to the Creator, it restores meaning to your life and answers the questions: Who am I? Where did I come from? And what is the purpose for my existence? At such a juncture, you become an asset to the Creator and humanity rather than a burden and a wanderer who is simply existing and passing through this world, singing "The Sweet By-and-By."[6] You will desire to make a contribution to life, leave an imprint such that when you leave the world, you will have left a legacy rather than a vacancy. You would then be in the class of men and women like Martin Luther King Jr., Mahatma Gandhi, Rosa Parks, Florence Nightingale, Abraham Lincoln, Mother Theresa, Myles Munroe, and Nelson Mandela.

Many others in biblical history, like Father Abraham, King David, Queen Esther, and Paul the Apostle, believed in the sovereignty of God and the sanctity of his creation. They believed in the narrative of a God who created man in his image and likeness (that is, to have his nature, in terms of character and functionality). No wonder their memories live in the annals of history and more importantly in the hearts of men and women of valor. Abraham Lincoln will never lose his place in history because in 1863 he led the people of the United States of America to recognize God as supreme over the nation[7]. In recent memory (2019) Felix-Antoine Tshisekedi, President of the Democratic Republic of Congo, did the same when he dedicated the nation and its people into the hands of the Almighty God[8].

God is a manufacturer who is proud of his product—mankind. That explains why he gave humanity a written manual to live by—the scriptures. He has spare parts and a recovery plan should something go wrong with his product. His creation is full of wonders, beauty, and purpose.

According to his manual, God has an eternal purpose for the universe and mankind. This remains valid even in our generation (Proverbs 19:21). Our ignorance and misunderstanding may cause God to delay or change his plans, but they do not cancel his purpose to:

- ➤ Extend his heavenly governing system from the invisible to a visible colony called earth
- ➤ Create and commission a royal family called mankind to rule over the earth
- ➤ Empower his royal family to establish kingdoms on earth and make them look like heaven
- ➤ Influence the earthly kingdoms from heaven through a father-son type of relationship and not through religion
- ➤ Establish a commonwealth of citizens, not religious members, who as ambassadors can represent the government of heaven on earth

Indeed, God had and has a great plan and purpose for his kingdom expansion, with mankind as sovereign ruler of the earth. To realize this plan, he had to begin before the beginning.

Chapter 2

The Beginning before the Beginning

I f the Creator began the beginning, then his pre-existence is unquestionable. We address him as God, which is not his name but rather a description of character. The word God denotes a self-existing, self-sufficient being. His existence precedes the creation of the universe because it is written in the book of Beginnings, which reads, "In the beginning, God created the heavens and the earth" (Genesis 1:1). This implies his existence before the beginning of creation, and his benevolence is actualized in the wonders of his creation.

Everything that exists today started as an idea in someone's mind. Ideas are thoughts which, when spoken, become words. Words are sound waves that can be converted into particles and are like dynamite (with the capacity and power to either create or destroy). The triune nature of God is manifested in creation through the power of thoughts and words. These thoughts and power were in him when he created the heavens—an invisible realm, otherwise called the spirit world. His first spoken thought became the Word. This spoken word, in unison with his power, created the visible realm—the universe, the planets and governing systems.[9]

Everything existed in God before he spoke them into existence (John 1:3). He created the heavens first, to be his domain with all spiritual beings (Psalm 33:6) and became the king of the invisible domain called the kingdom of heaven. He then conceived the idea of having a royal family and extending his kingdom authority and influence to another territory. This distant territory, called earth, would be governed by his family created in his image and likeness.

God's desire to have a royal family was the reason the physical realm was created and why he released his spiritual sons into the physical realms and made for them physical bodies. God is spirit, and his spiritual sons needed physical bodies to rule over planet earth. The spiritual sons in physical bodies, called mankind (humankind), were to make the earth look like their original home country—heaven. The earth, the governing systems and mankind would constitute the colony of the kingdom of heaven (Psalm 24:1). Hence to understand mankind and the universe, one has to take a trip backward into the mind of the Creator to understand his intention for creation. The seen world proceeded from the unseen, as it is written, "For the things which are seen are temporary, but the things which are not seen are eternal" (2 Corinthians 4:18).

Moses caught a revelation of the creation of the universe, including the galaxies, and documented them in the book of

Genesis. The earth is millions of years old, but the governing systems upon it are as old as the first human beings (Genesis 1:26). In this technological advanced world, we are mesmerized by how someone thousands of years ago could describe the events of creation that occurred millions of years before he was born. Moses documented the past, present and future. His narrative regarding the creation of mankind and purpose for existence can only be described as a wonder and mystery. The Creator must have given him a 'godoscope or spiriscope' to view the spiritual and then explain the extension of the physical from the spiritual. This can only be the case because microscopes and telescopes can only help us see and understand the physical.

Tighten your seat belt as we journey along to discover how the creation story unfolded and what happened thereafter.

God's perfect creation of the heavens and earth were narrated by Moses in Genesis 1:1: "In the beginning God created the heavens and the earth." Shockingly, in the second verse of the same chapter he records a universal disaster. "The earth was without form and void and darkness was on the face of the deep." The rest of the chapter narrates how God restored the earth before giving his spiritual sons physical bodies to rule over it (Genesis 1:2–25).

This disaster that shattered the earth is the pivot on which the wheels of creation and evolution keep revolving. There is no record regarding the number of years that separated the first and second verse in Genesis 1. It could have been millions to billions of years. Think about it: This could be the major confluence of science, archaeology, and theology. It could define the period between the perfect creation, the chaotic world, and its restoration to give us more hindsight and foresight on what is referred to as the "big bang theory." This theory describes the origin of all space, time, matter, and energy approximately 13.7 billion years ago from the violent expansion of a singular point of extremely high density and temperature.[10]

Theologians have worked tirelessly to demystify evolution against the backdrop of the big bang theory. Other religious folks and preachers have confused such efforts by handling the Bible as a religious book and trying to separate science from their religious beliefs.

The message of the Bible is not about a religion but a manufacturer's manual about a divine project to govern the earth from another place through mankind. It is a kingdom book, about a king, his kingdom, governing systems, royal family, colony, independence, and recolonization. In this manual, God summarizes his intention to extend his governing authority from the invisible realm (the celestial or home country) to the visible realm (the terrestrial or colony) to be administered by his royal family (mankind). He further explains how the colony declared independence from the home country and the recolonization program set in motion to restore it. In a nutshell, the entire message of the Bible is about government and governance.

The kingdom of heaven is God's sphere of governance. It is the headquarter of his sovereign rule. It existed long before mankind but extended to earth after God created Adam and

Eve. The earth was created as a colony of heaven and given to the first male and female as an inheritance to exercise their sovereign authority (Matthew 25:34). In honor of his creator, the greatest Old Testament king, David, made a remarkable statement in his book of praises, Psalms, saying, "The earth is the Lord's, and all its fullness, the world and those who dwell therein" (Psalm 24:1). In Psalm 115, David pulled away the curtain for us to see and understand the spheres of the two different governing authorities, one in heaven and the other on planet earth: "The heaven, even the heavens, are the Lord's; but the earth He has given to the children of men" (v. 16). This psalm differentiates the earth and its fullness (non-living and living creatures) from the world (governing systems) and all who dwell in it (mankind).

Colonization is not man's idea but God's. The Creator intended to extend his governing authority and resources from his "commonwealth bank" in heaven to the earth, in order to make the world function just like heaven, with the right governing systems, justice, peace and prosperity for all. When humanity lost God's concept of colonization, things turned ugly. Instead of the kingdom of heaven's model of governing the world, mankind invented corrupt kingdoms and colonies of shame and destruction—people dominating one another, colonial masters exploiting colonies, failed states, religious confusion, and global anarchy. This is not God's pattern and intent for colonization.

Chapter 3

The Creation of Man and the Making of Mankind

Amasterpiece of the Creator, man comes in two models—male and female; has three components, body, soul and spirit as referenced in scripture (1 Thessalonians 5:23). The spirit is God conscious, the soul self-conscious, while the body is world conscious. These components—'trinity', give them the ability to relate with their Creator, self, and the environment.

God is Spirit and wanted a family, so he created man in his image and likeness. In this regard, humans are spirit beings like their source. This "spirit man" existed in God before the creation of the world. When the first spirit man was released to the earth, God formed for him a *hu*mus body, and he became a living being (*human* being). Humans are, therefore, the greatest crowning achievement of God. They were created from the unseen realm and given bodies from the seen realm and commanded to dominate the seen realm with authority from the unseen. Man, therefore, operates in two kingdoms and is expected to live by two constitutions: one from the original country (heaven) and the other from the natural country (earth).

The spirit man became human beings when God made for them bodies from the humus soil. Like all spirits, the spirit man was neither male nor female, since spirits have no gender. In making the body for the spirit man, God decided to make two models: one male and the other female. He made or formed the first body from the humus soil and put in it one spirit man and called this model male. He later put the male into a deep sleep, pulled out a rib from his side, cloned and fashioned it into a female body, and put into it another spirit man (Genesis 2:21). He now had two individuals whom we may refer to as male man and the female man. The first was named Adam and the second Eve. The difference between the male and female were in structure and function.

The female man has a *womb*, hence called a *woman*, and because she can carry a *fetus*, we call her *female*. Their differences were not for competition but complementarity. God's purpose required these two genders working together in cooperation to accomplish a mutual vision.

God gave them one vision, a physical assignment to dominate the earth and make it function like heaven. Therefore, mankind is the only creation that has to live circumspectly, obeying both natural and spiritual laws (Ephesians 5:15). When God talks to mankind, he is talking to the man inside the body that is neither male nor female. Animals on the other hand, cannot pick up God because they have no spirits and live within the realms of natural and social laws, which is why praying is not natural to them, even though some may be trained to perform religious rituals.

Humans are spirits in bodies, they are the only legal spirits on the earth. According to divine principles any spirit operating on earth without a body is illegal. So, when God said to the male and female, "Let them have dominion…," he was legally separating himself from the environment called earth because he is a spirit without a body. Spirits are immortal but bodies are not. When the body dies the spirit must leave because it becomes illegal and has to return to God (Ecclesiastes 12:7).

The spirit man originated from God who is Spirit and their physical bodies were made for them in the resident country, called earth, to impact it with the culture of the home country. They were born of God and given citizenship of the kingdom of heaven and made ambassadors on earth, to represent the government of the home country. Their children, by the law of inheritance, were expected to be born citizens of heaven and ambassadors on earth. When Adam and Eve lost their citizenship, their offspring needed to have a re-birth to regain their heavenly citizenship in order to reign on earth again.

Humanity's loss of connection with their home country led them to become like shooting stars that travel at high speed without much control or direction. Instead of complementing one another, confusion became the order of the day.

What was meant to unite them became a dividing factor that gave birth to competition and irresponsibility. However, deep in the human soul is the yearning for the home country and its culture, which lies dormant waiting for an opportunity to bounce back.

Chapter 4

The Creation of the Colony

The earth and the governing systems were created for a purpose. The Creator wanted to extend his kingdom from the invisible to a visible realm. Planet earth and the systems upon it became the Creator's most important "outpost," which can be referred to as the colony of the kingdom of heaven.

A colony is a distant territory governed by a king from a distant kingdom. The people in the territory are cultured to live, talk, and act like the king in the home country. If you visit a colony, you can perceive the values, morals, attitudes, and culture of the kingdom without visiting it.

God placed his royal family in the colony and gave them authority over the governing systems in accordance with his Word: "The heaven, even the heavens, are the Lord's; But the earth has He given to the children of men" (Psalm 115:16).

As a loving and benevolent king, God wanted mankind to enjoy dominion. The keywords in the transfer of authority from God to man, so that man can experience kingship were, "Let them have dominion" (Genesis 1:26). In the concepts of royalty and kingdoms, a son can only become king when the king dies or abdicates the throne. Given that God and his throne are eternal, he decided to create another territory, unlike his, for his offspring to rule and reign as kings.

In life, planning should precede procreation. This is a divine concept that God displayed when he decided to create the earth, with all its life-sustaining trees, animals, water, and other underground resources, before releasing man from the invisible realm. After he had created all things on the earth and saw that they were good, he then made the male and female. He stationed them in the garden of Eden as the custodians and stewards of the colony.

The garden was the first colonial headquarters of the kingdom of heaven on earth and was expected to expand and cover the entire globe. All was well in Eden. During the cool of the day, God would come visit the first parents of all humans—Adam and Eve (Genesis 3:8). Like their source, this couple had infinite wisdom and creative abilities. They were able to discern the nature of all the animals and named them accordingly.

Adam and Eve enjoyed their work and perhaps discussed how to start their own family according to divine principles of reproduction, whereby they would take on the responsibility of providing a body for the spirit man to dwell. The male produces the spermatozoa and the female, the ovum. When the sperm and egg meet, a body is formed into which God infuses the spirit man. The male is equipped with a sexual delivery system, while the female has a sexual receptive system to receive the spermatozoa. The mother's womb incubates the products of conception into a body, boy or girl. The man has the seed while the woman is the incubator. Scripture holds that Adam and Eve lived in God's presence and had a "divine partnership" with the Creator to bring forth other humans to planet earth so they could be trained to extend the culture of heaven throughout the earth.

The spirit man originated from the source or father in the home country, fatherland, and were conversant with divine concepts, including speaking the language of the home country—the words or tongues of God. The Creator did not have to go to the earth to form a body for every spirit man coming to the earth. The male and female took on this responsibility, and the female became the sole incubator of the fetus and birth of other human beings on earth. In honor of motherhood, we call our planet "mother earth" and our first language our "mother tongue."

Adam and Eve knew their origin and purpose on earth and had all the materials needed to perform their divine assignment to make the earth function just like heaven— the home country. Responsibility existed between both of them. Adam was given the responsibility to teach and lead his wife by virtue of the fact that he was made first and instructed on what to do before Eve appeared on the scene.

Eve, on the other hand, had the greater responsibility to assist Adam to achieve the divine assignment. They were like head and neck: The head gives directions while the neck helps to turn the head. Without the neck turning, the man would eventually have a "stiff neck." They understood the purpose of everything God made available to them. To say the least, our first parents had a great and noble relationship with one another and, above all, with their Creator and maker.

Chapter 5

The Fall of Satan—A Coup D'état in Heaven

It is written, "In the beginning God created the heavens and the earth" (Genesis 1:1). The question that runs through one's mind is, if the Creator is a God of order and perfection, how come the world he created went chaotic in the second verse of the same chapter? It reads, "The earth was without form and void; and darkness was upon the face of the deep…" Something terrible must have occurred to warrant the disorder, void and darkness that engulfed the earth.

Ezekiel, an Old Testament prophet, gave insight into some of the events that led up to the chaos of the world. He spoke of a rebellion in heaven—the overthrow of the perpetrators and their expulsion to planet earth. A coup d'état had taken place in heaven. The coup leader was none other than Lucifer (afterward called the devil). The prophet Ezekiel referred to him as the king of Tyre, and he was in charge of the garden of God

THE FALL OF SATAN—A COUP D'ÉTAT IN HEAVEN

until iniquity was found in him, meaning he decided that he wanted to be God (Ezekiel 28). His position as worship leader and in-charge of God's garden in heaven gave him the craving for God's throne.

Lucifer gathered some angels and mounted a coup d'état against God's great army. The war that broke out in heaven and the consequences were also revealed in the Apocalypse of John, also called the book of Revelation: "And war broke out in heaven: Michael and his angels fought with the dragon; and the dragon and his angels fought, but they did not prevail, nor was a place found for them in heaven any longer. So the great dragon was cast out, that serpent of old, called Devil and Satan, who deceives the whole world; he was cast to the earth, and his angels were cast out with him" (Revelation 12:7–9).

The insurgence of the devil and his angels, in political terms, can be equated to the formation of a "terrorist organization" designed to remove the ruling party from power. The devil probably perceived that the ruler in heaven was planning to extend his governing authority to a colony and make mankind its administrator. He also could have been bitter that he was being left out of this arrangement, given that the offspring of the Creator would be kings, while he remained a mere angel or serving spirit. He forgot that the offspring were created from God to dominate the physical realm, while angels serve in the unseen.

When satan and his collaborators were finally cast out of heaven, he fell to earth like lightning. Jesus testified to the fall, saying, "I saw Satan fall like lightning from heaven" (Luke

10:18). Could such a statement and the prophecies by Ezekiel begin to narrow the gap between scientific and theological knowledge regarding the changes that have occurred in our universe?

The prophetic end time message to Daniel hints on such a scenario. "But you, Daniel, shut up the words, and seal the book until the time of the end; many shall run to and fro, and knowledge shall increase" (Daniel 12:4). The exponential increase in science and technology may someday lead scientists and cosmologists to help us understand if there are relations between the "lightning fall of Satan" from heaven to the earth, the big bang theory and the fragmentation of planet earth into what we call today the seven continents.

Nonetheless, the rebellion in heaven, the fall of satan and the destruction of God's orderly universe in Genesis 1:2 did not catch the Creator by surprise. It only altered his plans but not his purpose. The course of events set in motion a plan to re-establish and restore order to the earth as recorded in Genesis chapter 1, verses 3 to 21. Each recovery process begins with these words: "Then God said..."

This period is inadvertently referred to as the creation of the universe. This in fact was a rearrangement activity, where God separated and called forth things that had gone into disarray. He turned on the light to see the mess, gathered the waters into one place for the dry land to appear, then called forth grass, fruit trees and living creatures to multiply and fill the waters, earth and skies. He did this in five days, and when he saw that the earth had recovered its form and was as good as the original earth he had created in verse 1, he then formed mankind on the sixth day, and on the seventh day, God rested (Genesis 1:3-31; 2:2).

Recall that before the recovery process, man was still a spirit in the unseen realms without a physical body. God was putting everything in order to make sure all of man's needs were available before giving him a body. "And the Lord God formed man of the dust of the ground, and breathed into his nostrils the breath of life; and man became a living being" (Genesis 2:7). Hitherto, he was a living spirit. But as a living being, he had a spirit and body and was given a free will (soul).

Chapter 6

Treason in Eden—Rebellion
in the Colony

As God was re-arranging the earth, satan and his fallen
angels took abode in the firmament above the earth and
watched God at work. With his abode in the firmament, satan
became the prince of the power of the air (Ephesians 2:2) and
observed God as he formed the male and female. Satan could
have said to himself, "Although the Lord of Hosts prevailed over
the rebellion in heaven, he will have to deal with another on
earth." His plan was to deceive man and lead them to commit
treason by rebelling against their Creator, thereby declaring independence from the home country.

For his plan to materialize, satan needed a physical body
to be legal and operate on earth. He conceived a plan to borrow the body of the serpent, which explains why he is sometimes referred to as the old serpent. His deception worked and
he moved into Eden, just at a moment when the woman was

separated from the man, for whatever reason. He offered Eve what they already had, God's image and likeness, when he said, "You will not surely die. For God knows that the day you eat of it your eyes will be opened, and you will be like God, knowing good and evil" (Genesis 3:4–5). A seed of doubt was sown, and consequently mankind started to doubt their self-identity, their source, and purpose in life. They forgot the reality that they were created in God's image and likeness and did not need affirmations from the wrong source.

That event marked the beginning of the fall of mankind. They rebelled against their Creator and lost their birthrights to a fallen angel. Satan knew God would not intervene, given that God is faithful to his word. He had decreed, "Let them have dominion on the earth." By so doing, God legally separated himself from interfering with whatever choices Adam and Eve would decide to make.

Satan was ignorant of God's alternate plan—"Plan B," should man fall into temptation. One can imagine, before releasing man to earth, the holy Trinity met, as a follow-up to their earlier meeting when God said, "Let Us make man in Our image, according to Our likeness" (Genesis 1:26). In the conversation the three-in-one, God the Father, Son and Holy Spirit, checked on the possibility of satan insinuating a rebellion against their agenda. The Holy Spirit could have asked the Father what he would do if mankind rebelled against him. The Son may have replied that he would take on a human form, move to the earth, and die to pay the death penalty the Father would pronounce on the man and woman should they disobey and eat of the tree of knowledge and evil: "You shall not eat, for in the day that you eat you shall surely die" (Genesis 2:17).

Once the Son narrated the salvation plan, the Holy Spirit wrote in the minutes, "The Lamb slain from the foundation of the world" (Revelation 13:8). When the Son took on human form and finally arrived on earth, he testified of his decision, saying, "Therefore the Father loves Me, because I lay down My life that I may take it again. No one takes it from me, but I lay it down of Myself" (John 10:17–18). This is the story of the great exchange, the divine alternate plan that occurred on Calvary more than two thousand years ago.

God announced and recorded his Plan B in the book of Genesis, thousands of years before its manifestation: "And I will put enmity between you and the woman, And between your seed and her Seed. He shall bruise your head and you shall bruise His heel" (3:15). In other words, God made arrangements to prepare a body for himself in the womb of a young virgin, so he could descend to the earth legally and face the devil head-on. "Therefore the Lord Himself will give you a sign: Behold, the virgin shall conceive and bear a Son, and shall call his name Immanuel" (Isaiah 7:14).

This prophecy hinted at God's plan of redemption, which would be manifested in the fullness of time. In the meantime, God's purpose of heaven on earth would come to pass regardless. His sovereign agenda for human government would surely come to the earth. He laid his restoration or recovery plan in the Old Testament using a prototype nation called Israel. Even though his plan kept changing, his ultimate purpose remained. Let's watch God at work.

Chapter 7

The Lost Colony and Consequences—The Clash of Two Kingdoms in the Same Colony

Adam and Eve's disobedience and fall from dominion resulted in the loss of their God-given governing influence over the earth. After which, an illegal governing authority, led by satan, was established. Our first parent's divine mandate to govern and dominate the earth, and make it look like heaven was lost when they disobeyed God and declared independence from the home country. Thus the "human independence flag" was raised in the colony while the "heavenly kingdom flag" was simultaneously lowered until humanity was severed from the king and his kingdom.

As per colonial principle, once a colony declares independence from the home country, the governor sent from the home country is recalled with immediate effect. Likewise, when Adam and Eve declared independence from heaven's governing authority, the governor, who is the King's Spirit that lived inside them, was recalled. He was the very essence of life in mankind, the foundation of self-government, what we may call self-policing.

After the fall, the Holy Spirit left, and they transitioned from depending on spiritual consciousness to soulish and external consciousness. Humanity began to depend on the soul (mind, will and emotions) and the five senses to interpret life. From then on, what was seen, heard, touched, tasted, and smelled became the dominant components in the human journey of life. The wonderful gifts of intelligence and science lost their rightful position; we started using them to try and figure out who we are and not.

The consequences of the rebellion were dramatic and are still reverberating in our current world. Humanity had ventured into uncharted waters. They had lost the governor and a perfect governing system, which resulted in bad governance and all the problems experienced in the world today. The craving for good governance spans the globe, which is understandable because it is what man lost. Humankind never lost heaven but its governing systems. Nations spend billions of dollars to change governments but ignore the root cause of all their dysfunctions.

The righteous government Adam and Eve inherited from their King was intended to make them and their descendants live from the inside out (self-discipline) and depend on the source of all resources. Ever since the fall, mankind has tried to imitate the lifestyle of the kingdom they lost and have failed woefully—from relying on earthly kings and other leaders as their source to the establishment of religious institutions and other forms of government (communism, socialism, democracy), all which are failing.

Earthly kingdoms came into existence in the ancient past before the Middle Ages. Individuals who owned the land became known as "kings," and the territory over which the local king or landlord ruled, or exercised ownership rights and authority became their kingdoms. Everything on the land, including animals, natural resources, and all other materials, were considered personal property of the king. This system, also called feudalism, was God's original plan in Eden. The difference was that God intended for all men to be kings and lords on the earth, that is, not dominating other humans but ruling over animals, plants, birds, and sea creatures. This rulership mandate entailed good stewardship of all resources from the source.

As soon as man lost their authority, they lost their self-identity, self-worth, self-confidence, and Adam blamed his wife, instead of taking responsibility as head of the family. Their first son, Cain, murdered Abel his junior brother and became a fugitive. Irresponsibility, murder, and deception had replaced the government of righteousness, peace, and joy. Instead of the earth working for Adam and Eve, they had to struggle to provide for themselves. They started to run the planet without the king's nature, and this led to the breakdown of human authority and power to address vital issues. These actions morphed into the world's poverty, genocide, terrorism, political corruption, drug addiction and broken families.

The emptiness in human life is the absence of the governor, who connects us to our original home country and government. In his absence, we try to fill up the void with money, religion, relationships, sex, parties, drugs, work, and sports (or other forms of recreation).

Amid this chaos, God announced the return of the lost governing system, through the prophet Isaiah: "For unto us a Child is born. Unto us a Son is given; and the government will be upon His shoulder" (Isaiah 9:6). This restored government would ensure that every blessed nation had God as Creator and Lord, as foretold by King David, who ruled over Israel thousands of years before Jesus.

David wrote, "Blessed is the nation whose God is the Lord" (Psalm 33:12) to guide the judiciary, legislative and executive arms of government. This is in agreement with prophet Isaiah, who said, "For the Lord is our Judge, the Lord is our Lawgiver, the Lord is our King" (Isaiah 33:22). This is crucial, given that the world is searching for leaders who are connected to the government of the home country, like King David and Solomon. These kings wore two hats at the same time—a turban (priesthood) and a crown (kingship). They were spiritual and royal, a priest and king. King David's model of governing was a shadow of the coming King, Jesus, and the new governing system. That is why Jesus is often referred to as the son of David.

In anticipation of the full manifestation of the kingdom government, current governments must advocate for political, social, and spiritual justice. Governments should come to the realization that as sin precedes crime, spiritual justice should then precede political and social justice. That is judging circumstances based on God's position. The Bible is spot-on regarding the type of government the Messiah would bring upon his shoulder, one of peace and justice (Isaiah 9:7). This, however, begins with the acceptance of God's recolonization program, which will re-establish or reclaim the kingdom of heaven—his original governing system—on earth.

Jesus brought the government of heaven back to earth. This government called the kingdom of heaven is yet to be fully manifested in all spheres of life and nations of the world. The erratic and costly change of governments by nations is an indication of the yearning for a perfect government. Until we embrace the heavenly government, the wars over territory, injustice, inequality, and slavery will continue.

Chapter 8

God's Recolonization Plan

The written Word of God tells the story of the rise and fall of God's governing authority on earth and the master plan to regain it. The Bible—his "constitution"—has two well-documented sections: The Old and New Testaments. The Old Testament is the shadow or background information to the New Testament, which is the substance or true essence of the return of the kingdom of heaven to the earth. The two sections inform the readers of God's divine plan to recover his lost colony.

Journey to Recover the Lost Colony

The main theme throughout the document is the preparation and announcement of the coming king and the restoration of the heavenly government upon the earth. In it are accounts of kings, kingdoms, laws, prophets and stories of great men and women who heard and obeyed the voice of God. It has been postulated that the Old Testament is the New Testament concealed, and the New is the Old Testament revealed. In other words, the Old Testament writings are facts and stories with hidden principles, whereas the New Testament contains parables with revealed principles.

Genesis 1 and 2 describe the establishment of God's earthly kingdom handed over to the first couple to rule and manage. Genesis 3 narrates how the couple committed treason and lost their mandate to govern the earth. The rest of the Old Testament records God's plan to regain that kingdom and restore it to its original state, using Israel as a prototype nation to all the nations of the world.

The manifestation of the recovery plan takes place in the New Testament, which has three main subsections:

➢ The four Gospels
➢ The Acts of the Apostles
➢ The Epistles

The Gospels capture the return of the kingdom government, Acts demonstrates its operations, while the Epistles highlight the lifestyle in the new government.

In brief, the story of the Old Testament is about the king initiating his restoration program. It began with the call of a man named Abram, whose descendants God would use to build a nation of people he would call his own and by whom he would later send his Son to the earth to re-establish his lost kingdom. The call of Abram, who was later renamed Abraham, was the beginning of the recovery plan and establishment of a great nation that would be a prototype of what the kingdom of heaven on earth was supposed to look like.

The Call of Abraham

It has earlier been stated that God is spirit, and spirits cannot operate on earth without bodies. Should God desire to do anything on earth, he would need to either have a body or use man. God planned for both scenarios to salvage his lost colony, and he started with the latter—using man. Hence the call of Abram in Genesis chapter 12.

Biblical history informs us of how God called Abram out of his family and country to a land he promised to give him and his descendants forever (Genesis 12:1). When Abram believed God's promise to make him a father of a great nation, and a blessing to all the families of the earth, he became a friend and confidant of God. From that time onward, God changed his name from Abram to Abraham.

The call of Abraham was unique because God is a God of generations. He knew Abraham was a man who would obey him and teach his descendants to do likewise. The testimony of God concerning Abraham, and his calling, is documented in the Old Testament: "For I have known him, in order that he may command his children and his household after him, that they keep the way of the Lord, to do righteousness and justice, that the Lord may bring to Abraham what he has spoken to him" (Genesis 18:19). God had promised thus, "Abraham shall surely become a great and mighty nation, and all the nations of the earth shall be blessed in him" (v. 18).

In keeping with his promise, God made Abraham the father of a prototype nation (Israel) and gave him and his descendants an estate to manage, the promised land of Canaan. Israel, his natural seed, would set the pace for the coming of Jesus, the spiritual Seed. Jesus would be conceived in the womb of a woman from the house of one of his natural seed, the house of Judah. "Therefore, the Lord Himself will give you a sign: Behold, the virgin shall conceive and bear a Son, and shall call his name Immanuel," meaning "God with us" (Isaiah 7:14).

God did not hide his end-time game plan from his friend Abraham. God told him to offer his only son Isaac as a sacrifice to him. He obeyed God and took his only son, Isaac, to sacrifice him to the Lord. On their way, Isaac asked his father the where about of the lamb for the burnt offering. And Abraham said, "My son, God will provide for Himself the lamb for a burnt offering. So the two of them went together" (Genesis 22:8).

On the mountain in the land of Moriah, as Abraham was about to sacrifice Isaac, God provided a lamb as a sacrifice in the place of Isaac. "And God said to Abraham, do not lay your hand on the lad, or do anything to harm him; for now I know that you fear God, since you have not withheld your son, your only son from Me. Then Abraham lifted up his eyes and looked, and there behind him was a ram caught in a thicket by its horns. So Abraham went and took the ram and offered it up as a burnt offering instead of his son" (Genesis 22:12–13).

This was a foreshadow of the Lamb of God highlighted in the New Testament when John the Baptist saw Jesus coming toward him and said, "Behold! The Lamb of God who takes away the sin of the world!" (John 1:29).

God's visions and promises can hardly be fulfilled by a single man or in one generation. His Word transcends generations, and those who are in tune with his Word cherish succession. Before Abraham died, he made sure he transferred all he knew, including the knowledge and reverence of the God he served to his son, Isaac, who passed it down to Jacob. Jacob, who was later renamed Israel, became the father of the twelve tribes of the model nation God intended to use to bless all the families of the earth.

Before Abraham passed into eternity, God had informed him that his seed (Israel) would go to a foreign land to be tested and enslaved but would eventually emerge stronger by the hand of a deliverer. God said to Abram, "Know certainly that your descendants will be strangers in a land that is not theirs, and will serve them, and they will afflict them four hundred years" (Genesis 15:13). Based on the relationship God and Abraham had, God revealed the things that were to come after his death to best prepare his descendants for the turbulent years that lay ahead.

Israel's Sojourn into and out of Egypt

The selling of Joseph the dreamer, as a slave to the Egyptian merchants, was a divine set up to fulfill what God had said to Abraham. The "dreamer boy" testifying to this said to his brothers, "But now, do not therefore be grieved or angry with yourselves because you sold me here; for God sent me before you to preserve life" (Genesis 45:5).

True to his word, after several years of slavery in Egypt, God raised up a man called Moses to deliver the nation of Israel from Egypt, not directly into the promised land, but across the Red Sea, into the wilderness of Arabia.

A wilderness is usually a place of divine provision and transformation. Every delivered slave needs provisions to survive while acquiring the knowledge, skills, and abilities to live without a master. In other words, a delivered people need mental transformation to be free. However, Israel was ungrateful. Instead of remembering how God had delivered them from slavery and drowned Pharaoh's army in the Red Sea, they murmured, complained, and wished for the cucumbers, onions, and garlic in Egypt. All the children of Israel that left Egypt into the wilderness perished without crossing the Jordan river into Canaan, except Joshua and Caleb: "For the Lord had said to them, they shall surely die in the wilderness; So there was not left a man of them, except Caleb the son of Jephunneh and Joshua the son of Nun" (Numbers 26:65).

God allowed the rebellious generation in the wilderness to live for forty years to bring forth the next generation out of them, with a different mindset worthy of entering the promised land. This is the generation that Joshua led across the Jordan into the promised land, as it is written, "The carcasses of you who have complained against Me shall fall in this wilderness, all of you who were numbered, according to your entire number, from twenty years old and above. Except for Caleb the son of Jephunneh and Joshua the son of Nun, you shall by no means enter into the land which I swore I would make you dwell in. But your little ones, whom you said would be victims, I will bring in, and they shall know the land which you have despised" (Numbers 14:29–31).

God allowed Israel to wander in the wilderness for forty years because he wanted the Egyptian culture replaced with his own. The Egyptian traits and mentality that the children of Israel had grown accustomed to had to be flushed out! God did not want the Egyptian culture to be carried into the promised land, so his people would not be defiled or contaminated. And so, he fed them with manna and quails from heaven, and most importantly gave them the Ten Commandments and other ritual laws. These laws were to cause Israel to have a different lifestyle, one intended to prepare them for the return of the kingdom of heaven that Adam and Eve lost. This lifestyle was also designed to awaken Gentile nations to see the works of God and start admiring and desiring the return of the new government.

Moses, the Law, and the Prophets

The laws of Moses and the prophets in the Old Testament that were used to govern Israel were shadows of the righteous governing system Adam lost. The purpose of the laws and other rituals were to prepare Israel for the coming king. The prophets' key assignment was to announce the coming king and his mission to keep the people in perspective and their hope alive. The Ten Commandments written on tablets of stone were a shadow of the law of righteousness that would be written in the hearts of men.

The King's mission was to restore his people to the position they had fallen from—a position where they would have his written laws in their hearts, even as it is written, "Behold, the days are coming, says the Lord, when I will make a new covenant with the house of Israel and with the house of Judah—not according to the covenant that I made with their fathers in the days that I took them by the hand to lead them out of the land of Egypt, My covenant which they broke; ... But this covenant that I will make with the house of Israel after those days, says the Lord: I will put My law in their minds, and write it on their hearts; and I will be their God, and they will be My people." (Jeremiah 31:31–33)

Israel kept the Ten Commandments in the ark of the covenant and offered sacrifices of the blood of lambs for the remission of their sins. During these sacrificial ceremonies, the spirit of God would come upon the prophets to inform the kings and the priests to correct themselves so they could correct the nation, and the nation of Israel could then correct the nations of the world, for the ultimate purpose of redeeming the whole earth. As they continuously broke the law, and never listened to the prophets, the prototype nation was then excluded from the next phase of the plan for the complete restoration of the kingdom of God on the earth. Though the nation of Israel was excluded, God still worked with a chosen few through whom his contingency plan for the world would take effect.

God had to execute the next phase of his contingency plan of acquiring a body and coming to earth to redeem the world and his royal family (John 1:14; Hebrews 10:5). He had to put his Word (Son) in a body, called Immanuel. The Son would not cancel the law and the prophets but would fulfill them (Matthew 5:17). He would return the convicting spirit into the law, which would explain the intention behind the laws, which the religious leaders had turned into a religion.

Chapter 9

A New Government
Sent to the Colony

The purpose of the King's Son coming into the world was to salvage it and its inhabitants from the control of the prince of darkness—the devil. This prince had corrupted the entire governing system, its values and culture. Even the earth was groaning under the yoke of his corrupted influence.

The rightful heirs—humans, lost authority over the earth and mastery of natural forces. Consequently, earthquakes, storms, volcanic eruptions, and plagues wreaked havoc on humans, animals, and aquatic life. The earth that humans were created and made to dominate started dominating them. Uncontrolled and unbridled emotions led mankind into various kinds of perversion.

The fall from dominion deprived mankind of self-discipline and self-government. Institutions of governance and laws to this day are unable to regulate human behavior. Lawmakers set themselves above the law, and the commoners are weighed down by the very laws that are supposed to protect them. In the beginning of creation this was not meant to be so. The Creator never intended that mankind be governed by external institutionalized governments with written rules and regulations. God's intent was and remains self-government, with his laws written in the hearts of mankind.

Failing states, national upheavals, plagues, religious confusion, and global anarchy are virtually bringing mankind to their knees to acknowledge the fact that humanity needs help from somewhere else. "We cannot solve our problems with the same thinking we used when we created them."[11] Humanity needs a system of government that is out of this world, one of peace and justice (Isaiah 9:6–7). This is the system Jesus the Son of God—the male man, brought upon his shoulders into the world.

Jesus, the Male Man!

The Creator of the universe cherishes integrity, abhors lawlessness, and loves order. The first spirit man he formed a body for was a male, called Adam (Genesis 2:7). Adam was the first son of God in a human body (Luke 3:38). God gave him the instructions regarding what he wanted to happen on the earth, then handed over to him the authority to govern and dominate it before Eve was formed. Adam, therefore, became the head of the human family and by default the first line of authority in the colony. In that light, whatever happened, right or wrong, concerning the dominion mandate in the colony was squarely upon his shoulders.

The fall of the human race can therefore be referred to as a "male problem" and needed males to head and lead the restoration agenda. Not to sound condescending, but purpose defines assignment. God delegated authority on earth to the males and purposed the females to influence the males so that both genders, working together, would accomplish God's vision.

Satan understood the chain of command and the dynamics of the male authority and female influence and used the female to influence the male. The temptation in Eden was targeted toward Adam and not Eve. Eve was successfully manipulated into influencing Adam to disobey God, and as a result, the human family fell from dominion.

Despite the lapse of judgment on the woman's part, God still had a plan to use her as a portal for his Son into the world to crush satan's head. Though males are at the center of God's recovery plan, the females are the incubators and influencers of every divine move. Every male coming to the earth, except Adam, is born of a woman, even Jesus.

According to Scripture, Jesus was referred to as the second or last Adam (1 Corinthians 15:45) born of a virgin of the house of Judah. Since the first Adam was male and the fall of man attributed to him, Jesus by default had to be male to champion the redemption plan, as it is written, "For as by one man's disobedience many were made sinners, so also by one Man's obedience many will be made righteous" (Romans 5:19).

Before the fullness of time, God had to speak through men and established a covenant with Abraham. Through his descendants, God's Son would be born to save the world. This intricate plan involved Abraham because it was through his seed that the birth of Jesus would be fulfilled. Thus, Jesus was born a Jew by default to redeem the promise made to Abraham, the father of the Jewish nation—Israel.

Had the call of Abraham been made to an Asian or African, Jesus would have been either Asian or African. Therefore, Jesus became male and a Jew by virtue of the fact that the first Adam was male, and the promise of a savior was given to Abraham. Furthermore, Jesus's choice of the twelve apostles, all of whom were male, was intended to address the male problem. However, Jesus understood the power of females to influence the world, so he called his church his bride, not bridegroom, as referenced by Paul in Scripture (Ephesians 5:25–27).

Jesus (body) made Christ (Spirit) legal on earth and hence he was called Jesus the Christ, Son of Man and Son of God. The body of Jesus, the child, was prepared in the womb of the virgin to house the Son, as it is written, "For unto us a Child is born, unto us a Son is given" (Isaiah 9:6). The child referring to Jesus, while the Son to Christ.

The use of terminologies in biblical narratives quite often obscure understanding. Words like *man, son, father, church,* and the pronouns *he* or *she* ascribed to them, go unnoticed but provide valuable information concerning the beings.

The word *man* denotes a spirit in a body that has a soul. Man has no gender, hence is not a she, he, him, or her. God is Spirit and not a sexist. When he is talking to man, he is addressing the spirit man inside the bodies of the male and female. Inadvertently, we ascribe the pronouns he and him to God and his triune nature—Father, Son and Holy Spirit—overlooking the fact that these are spirits and spirits have no gender. However, the bodies prepared for the spirit man on earth have genders that are intended to fulfill the purpose of God.

The word *Father* means "source" while Son refers to "offspring." This does not relate to the identity of the male. God, in his infinite wisdom, used the word *father* to address the male in the family and the pronoun *he* was then adapted to refer to God and the male man. Similarly, we have come to refer to heaven, our original home country, as fatherland and the earth, our resident country, as motherland or mother earth.

With this understanding, addressing God the Father, his Son and Spirit as he or him and the church as she is not discriminatory and should not be considered a gender issue. The genealogy of Jesus as a Jew should not also be interpreted as a racial bias. Neither should the fact that his disciples were all males be considered and deemed unfairness to the female gender. The assignment at stake needed the fronting of males to address the male problem while the females supported the agenda because they had unmatched and unprecedented power to influence. There was a need for the two genders to work together in the garden of Eden, and that need has not changed. It is therefore no coincidence that the King's Son, Jesus, was born to a woman of Jewish decent, in Bethlehem of Judah (Luke 1:30–31; Matthew 2:1–2).

The Birth of the King's Son

The birth of the King's Son and his purpose were announced in Genesis and later prophesied by Moses and many Old Testament prophets, notably Isaiah. At the fullness of time, God sent an angel, called Gabriel, to announce the conception and birth of a child to a young virgin in Nazareth. This was unprecedented; such a conception had never occurred in human history. The Son was born at the appropriate time when Palestine was under the colonial rule of the Roman Empire. He was born a king and not a prince because his Father had ordained him to be born into another territory, the earth, to enjoy kingship.

The best narrative of the virgin conception and birth of Jesus is documented in the book written by Luke, who was a medical doctor and a disciple of Jesus. It is suggested that Luke was the family doctor of Mary and Joseph, the earthly father of Jesus. In the Gospels, Luke informs us that the Holy Spirit came upon Mary and she conceived and bore a child, who would save the world from sin. By inference, Jesus was the King's Son sent from heaven into the colony.

The conception of Jesus by the Holy Spirit was in keeping with God's promise and kingdom principles. Jesus, provided a body for the Holy Spirit to dwell in, because without a body the Holy Spirit was illegal on earth. Ultimately the birth of Jesus ushered the return of the governor who had been recalled when the colony declared independence.

We should bear in mind that the birth of Jesus was the fulfillment of God's promise made to the devil after he instigated a rebellion against God in the garden of Eden. This subsequently led to the declaration of independence by the colony and the recall of the Governor—the Holy Spirit. The Governor took legal residence in the person of Jesus throughout his earthly ministry. The miracles Jesus performed as he "returned in the power of the Spirit to Galilee, and news of Him went out through all the surrounding region" (Luke 4:14). These wonders were the handiworks and evidence of the presence of the Holy Spirit, and Jesus testified of them, saying that by himself he could do nothing. He only did what he heard and saw the Spirit of the Father say and do.

For Jesus to deliver the Spirit of God, resident in him to his followers, he had to die, resurrect, ascend into heaven, and then send the Spirit back to earth. This would be the master plan of God's redemptive work of salvation. Jesus' death would pay the penalty of humanity's rebellion and make their bodies worthy to host the Holy Spirit once again (John 12:23–24; 20:22; Acts 1:4).

Born in the Fullness of Time

From Adam to the birth of Jesus was approximately four thousand years. God made sure everything lined up before sending his Son. This involved the rise of the Roman Empire with some characteristics of God's kingdom concept of colonization. The Roman Empire was the most powerful and successful kingdom in history, from Africa to Scotland, because they used God's idea of colonization. Instead of carrying people from a captured territory to Rome, they brought Rome to the territory. God used the timing of the Roman occupation of Palestine to send Jesus because everything he would say would be understood to avoid misconception and misinterpretation.

At this point in time, God continued to redeem his promise to Abraham and in so doing raised up a forerunner, John the Baptist, to proclaim the return of the kingdom of heaven to the earth. God was restoring his governing authority from heaven to the earth in order that the earth would be just like heaven. Therefore, anyone praying to escape to heaven is not in sync with God's Word.

Jesus did not come to take mankind to heaven but to restore heaven's governing authority to earth. The recolonization program was well on its way and from that time forward, Jesus began to preach and to say, "Repent for the kingdom of heaven is at hand" (Matthew 4:17). In other words, the culture and way of life in the kingdom of heaven had returned to earth, and people were to change their thinking patterns and lifestyle and start living as God intended.

Chapter 10

Jesus Establishes a Political Agenda

The existing "ruling party" in the colony was set up by satan and his cronies. Satan assumed rulership as the prince of the power of the air and lord of darkness, and influenced the colony's political, economic, and social systems. He was a formidable force that was well entrenched in the fabric of society. A strategy backed by divine authority and power was required to overthrow this illegal government in the colony.

Jesus established an "opposing party" with a clear political agenda to counter the illegal authority. This agenda included: a succinct manifesto, effective and efficient governing principles and structures, strategies with key directions and expected results, campaign structures and financial modalities with mentoring and succession plans. As the leader of the divine "opposition," he had all these put together to take the devil head-on. All was set for the launch of the campaign to restore order to the colony. As was expected, the devil would bruise his heel, but he would bruise his head and make a public spectacle of him and his fallen angels (Genesis 3:15; Colossians 2:15).

The Manifesto

In his first public engagement, Jesus, being empowered from above, went straight to the point. He publicly pronounced his mission statement, saying, "The kingdom of Heaven has returned; Repent" (Matthew 4:17 paraphrased). In essence, he was saying the governing system that man lost had returned to earth, so people should change their way of thinking. He then reiterated his Father's mandate, which underlined the kingdom's intent for his assignment: "For God so loved the world that He gave his only begotten Son, that whoever believes in Him should not perish but have everlasting life" (John 3:16). This was the beginning of his campaign against the corrupt ideologies of the devil.

The fall produced a different ideology from God's original idea for man to rule and dominate the earth. Christ was God's collective ideas in the flesh—Jesus (John 1:1, 14), purposed to counteract the diabolic ideology of the fallen systems on earth. The dire situation at hand necessitated a spiritual redemption and a mental transformation. It required one laying down his life for the introduction of a new ideology. Jesus testified to this by saying, killing him would only make his kingdom multiply, even as a grain of wheat does (John 12:24; 2:19). His type of politics was not a popular uprising but rather revolutionary, whereby the leader lays down his life for the cause, rather than the people dying for it (John 10:11; 18:8). This is unlike present-day politics, where political leaders use people to achieve their ambitions, a true reflection of the fallen mentality that satan introduced after man lost his divine nature.

The "terrorist government" of darkness ruled the colony. Satan along with his fallen angels influenced humanity, and they terrorized each other. This state of emergency called for one who would empower a new following, with an ideology that would neutralize evil. The Old Testament method of fighting them with ritual laws, swords, arrows, and spears had yielded no concrete results. It was like trying to stump out terrorism by bullets and bombs. Terrorism is a corrupt ideology that only God's idea of governance can counter.

The Principles

Jesus, on multiple occasions, narrated stories with principles embedded in them. Principles produce a culture that becomes a lifestyle. Kingdom citizens have authority to ask and receive their rights and privileges according to the will of God and the principles in his law (1 John 5:14).

The kingdom of heaven runs its operations on principles. Love is a cardinal pillar of the kingdom. It is the principle on which creation is founded. The Creator is love and likewise humans because we were created in his image and likeness. In that regard when God sees man, he sees himself. He therefore expects us to love one another regardless of creed, race, gender, color, and social status. Jesus summed up all of Gods laws in one word: love. That is why he said, "A new commandment I give you, that you love one another; as I have loved you" (John 13:34). The principle here is that of vertical love before horizontal love. Vertical love is love for God, whereas horizontal love is love for others. When you love God, He will give you the ability to love, forgive and care for yourself and others. Love, forgiveness, and compassion were prominent principles of Jesus' political menu.

The power of choice in man's will was another key principle Jesus underlined. Choice and free will indicated the love of God. God is love, and in loving his family, he gave them a free will to choose, even if it meant choosing against him. Jesus spoke of the consequences of violating principles with the power of our choices. We do not possess the power to pick and choose these consequences, they are inherent or inbuilt into natural and spiritual laws. They affect our relationship with God and the legacy we intend on leaving behind for our descendants. Moses communicated this to the nation of Israel, saying, "I have set before you life and death, blessing and cursing; therefore choose life, that you and your descendants may live" (Deuteronomy 30:19). And God reiterated a key consequence of wrong choices, saying, "Because you have forgotten the law of your God, I also will forget your children" (Hosea 4:6).

Jesus emphasized responsibility and the infallibility of God's Word. For peace to reign in the world, he admonished the fear of God, integrity, responsibility, and accountability. He himself was the Prince of Peace, and any peace and reconciliation platform or treaty without his Word taking precedence was bound to fail (1 Corinthians 3:11). The king's word is law to the citizens, and his disciples needed to understand that they could not debate or change it. On the contrary, religion is very flexible because people can debate, choose, and change to accommodate diverse agendas. Therefore, adherence to principles protects the bearer from the inherent consequences of violation and is vital to enjoying the rights and privileges of the kingdom while on earth.

Governing Structure

Jesus chose professionals, men who operated in diverse fields. They understood the ins and outs of business management, leadership, governance, and had no religious affiliations. Jesus gave them the assignment of building his government that would include a senate, cabinet and administration to extend the intentions of the king to families, communities, societies, and nations.

The governing board (apostles) established by Jesus was not a religious organization but a political entity. This board was created to lead the political assembly which Jesus called his church[12] or *ecclesia*, as opposed to the Greek version that gathered in Athens to debate policies.[13] Jesus himself was the head of the governing body with the task to overthrow and replace the existing tyranny led by satan. He demonstrated servant leadership and emphasized the philosophy of mentoring and "passing it on." Before his ascension into heaven he spoke to his disciples saying, "All authority has been given to Me, in heaven and on earth. Go therefore and make disciples of all nations, baptizing them in the name of the Father and of the Son and of the Holy Spirit, teaching them to observe all things that I have commanded you" (Matthew 28:18–20).

Mentoring and succession was crucial for the survival and success of the board's commission. Any form of corruption, manipulation, sectarianism, lies, force, coercion, and bribery were outlawed. Followers were to be attracted to the kingdom because of their understanding of the good news of the kingdom, and the lifestyle of those who had entered into it. Hence, the leadership success of the governing board was to be measured by the success of their successors.

Citizenship and Law

Like any other country, the kingdom of God has citizens, who are expected to abide by the law. Citizenship is the greatest gift a country can give anyone. It gives you rights and privileges that no foreigner, no matter how great, can have. Understanding kingdom citizenship has the power to attract people to it. Once people understand what it has to offer, they clamor to get in, just as people from poor nations are scrambling for citizenship of prosperous ones. Jesus highlighted this in the Gospels, saying, "The law and prophets were until John. Since that time, the kingdom of God has been preached, and everyone is pressing into it" (Luke 16:16).

Adam lost his citizenship and consequently all his children were born alien to the home country. Post redemption, upon receiving the revelation of their home of origin, the children become eligible to take an oath of allegiance, so that citizenship is bestowed upon them once again, akin to what Jesus described in the Gospels (Luke 22:29). This is the new birth (being born again) that makes us naturalized citizens of the kingdom of heaven and not members of religious organizations. Once we take the oath of allegiance and become citizens of God's kingdom, the repentance process of changing our mindset begins. We voluntarily align ourselves with a new government and new country, embracing its language, ideals, and values.

In God's kingdom all citizens carry dual citizenship, that of the kingdom of heaven as well as citizenship of the earthly nation. We do not give up our earthly citizenship when we become citizens of the kingdom of heaven. And in the same way, we do not have to be in heaven to benefit from heavenly jurisdiction. Our citizenship is constant, and the kingdom government exercises jurisdiction over us wherever we are.

The primary responsibility of any government is to take care of its citizens, whether at home or abroad, hence one of the main purposes of maintaining embassies. In the real sense, the church is an assembly of ambassadors who function as embassies of the kingdom of heaven and offer environments where citizens are trained in the laws, language, and culture of the kingdom of heaven for effective living in the colony—earth.

Citizens who love their country obey the law and maintain peace and order. Obeying the law makes you free in the country and gives you the right to enjoy all benefits. There is no freedom without the law. Man's primary citizenship is in heaven, but on earth they are ambassadors who represent the government of heaven and its political agenda.

As ambassadors, we are expected to do the following: focus on government affairs, understand our terms of reference in the recolonization mandate, request the king's will in the home country to manifest in the colony and be aware of the fact that all our needs are provided for by the home government so that we can tend to the kingdom government's business. We are not to compromise the home government's stand on issues but express its position only. This is why the disciples were mandated to make followers law abiding citizens of the kingdom of heaven and ambassadors of the new governing system. They were disallowed from participating or instigating political uprisings and chaos.

Petitioning in the Kingdom

Prayer is mankind exercising dominion on the earth by petitioning God to intervene in earth's affairs. It is seeking the will of the father to be done on earth through the return of his governing system. Mankind is the sole being that gives God the legal authority to intervene and establish his kingdom on earth. Jesus demonstrated its efficacy and advocated for it to be the heartbeat of all kingdom activities.

In response to the request made by the disciples, "Lord, teach us to pray as John taught his disciples" (Luke 11:1), Jesus prescribed the way citizens should approach the King in prayer and then proceeded to teach his disciples the model prayer (the "Lord's Prayer"): "Our Father in heaven, Hallowed be Your name, Your kingdom come, Your will be done on earth, as it is in heaven" (Luke 11:2). The disciples were then instructed to do the same with the assembly of believers.

Petitioning or prayer gives God the legality from heaven to intervene in our territory. Since God gave us authority over the earth, he requires the permission or authorization from mankind to act in it. Therefore, when we stop praying, we allow God's purposes for the world to be hindered, as satan and sin reign. Prayer is calling forth what God had already purposed and predestined.

Kingdom petitioning is and was a key instrument in the political assembly of Jesus. The disciples understood why they were called out of their jobs into their reason for existence (purpose). With this understanding of their purpose, prayer became a fundamental aspect of their divine assignment, to mobilize people of all nations to take up citizenship in the kingdom of heaven and together invoke the will of the king on the earth.

Rights and Privileges

Jesus said that he was giving those who believed in him as the Christ, the keys (laws and principles) of the kingdom (country of God). This is important because you access the rights and privileges from a country as a law-abiding citizen. The kingdom demands loyalty and obedience to the king, which is righteousness—a right standing with the king. Therefore, once you enter God's country you are commanded to keep the laws and all the rights and benefits are yours to enjoy.

God demands maturity and responsibility. Adam's irresponsibility caused him to hand over the earth's governing authority to the devil. Jesus came to transfer the governing mandate back to mankind, by taking the management deed from satan. Jesus, therefore, instructed his follower to preach or proclaim God's governing authority (gospel of the kingdom)—not theology or doctrines—because governance over the earth is what man lost.

Jesus never commanded his followers to construct buildings called churches but to build communities, because God desires to dwell in people and not in temples made with hands (Acts 7:48–50). The president of the United States of America had this to say regarding the church and the influence it has on the community: "Families and churches not government officials know best how to create a strong and loving community."[14] Communities make up countries, not buildings. The church therefore is an assembly of citizens, regardless of physical space, who are taught the laws of the kingdom from the king's constitution for effective living on earth. Any citizen who breaks the laws of the home country is put in a spiritual prison where rights and privileges are limited, akin to when national laws are broken. In a sense, Jesus reduced life to two words, *kingdom citizenship* and *righteousness*, when he said, "But seek first the kingdom of God and His righteousness, and all these things shall be added to you" (Matthew 6:33). Take up citizenship and have a right standing with the king to enjoy all spiritual and physical rights and privileges.

Reflections on the Sociopolitical and Religious Environment

The disciples were being sent out into harsh sociopolitical and religious terrains and needed to understand how to deal with the unexpected. Jesus underscored the fact that they were going out as sheep among wolves and could be easily devoured (Matthew 10:16).

Given that their mission to implement the political agenda of restoring the governing authority of the kingdom of heaven to the earth was political, they had to adhere and take into account several principles to arm and protect themselves from the existing political environment, the wrath of the religious leaders and the traditions of men. Some of the complex issues that needed sound judgement included human right approaches that would be beneficial to individuals, families, communities, and the nations. These rights were to hinge on personal responsibility and accountability.

The disciples were to respect all leadership, be it in families, communities, societies, and nations, because they were ordained by God. Any desire for change of leadership required petitioning the King in the home country to set the pace for change. They were not to instigate rebellion, "For rebellion is as the sin of witchcraft" (1 Samuel 15:23).

The modus operandi of the world's system is contrary to that of the kingdom of heaven. The disciples needed to understand that the world stage was under the influence of another authority and the vast majority got ahead any way they could by killing, hurting, and stealing. But the kingdom they represented had everything in reverse. To get ahead, they had to do the opposite of what the world was doing. Instead of receiving, they were to give; instead of hoarding, they were to release; instead of grabbing, they were to give up; instead of hating, they were to love; instead of "every man for himself," they were to show first regard to others.

They were to model the principle of lordship to the rest of the world. That is confessing Jesus, not only as Savior but also as Lord. They were to teach nations not only to acknowledge God as their Creator but to proclaim him as their Lord (owner). "For God did not send His Son into the world to condemn the world, but that the world through Him might be saved" (John 3:17). In other words, his disciples were not to become agents of condemnation but of love, compassion, and forgiveness.

They were to manifest the returned authority of the kingdom of heaven and were not to sacrifice to appease God to deliver, heal and bless anyone. Jesus instructed them to preach, saying, "The kingdom of heaven is at hand" (Matthew 10:7–8). They were to heal the sick, cleanse the lepers, raise the dead and cast out demons, because of the authority they had received.

Every vision has its provision; hence the disciples were to depend fully on the home government to provide all their needs. They were to provide neither gold nor silver for their journey for a worker is worthy of his food (vv. 9–10).

They were to remain true to their calling. They had the responsibility to ensure all converts looked upon and trusted in Christ whom God sent, as referenced in John 6:29, which reads, "This is the work of God that we believe in Him whom He sent."

The disciples were not left in the dark regarding the inheritance of the saints and the coming of the end, when all citizens will enjoy all their rights and privileges. As it is written, "And this gospel of the kingdom will be preached in all the world as a witness to all nations, and then the end will come" (Matthew 24:14). It will happen when nations start applying kingdom principles in all governing systems like education, economy, health, agriculture, and politics. In other words, when the kingdom culture becomes a lifestyle in all spheres of life, Jesus will return with a full-fledged governing system from heaven, whereby he will be the King of Kings and Lord of Lords (Revelation 19:16) and make us kings and priests to our God, and we shall reign on the earth (Revelation 5:10).

The sociopolitical and religious environments posed serious challenges to the outcomes of the kingdom message. Jesus never allowed his disciples to venture into their assignment without counsel regarding issues relating to citizens' rights and responsibilities, the world system's modus operandi, the lordship principle, kingdom manifestations, provision for every vision and the coming of the end. Such wise counsel was beneficial to the disciples as they went about implementing the political agenda of the kingdom of heaven. This is of great relevance today to ambassadors of the kingdom of heaven, who are working tirelessly to reclaim the Lord's lost colony.

Chapter 11

Strategic Directions to Reclaim the Colony

The chief architect, Jesus, called the establishment of heaven's government on earth his Father's business (Luke 2:49). Like any good businessman, he sought shrewd men from diverse backgrounds. This explains why he recruited all these professionals among whom were fishermen, like Peter, tax collectors, like Matthew, accountants, like Judas Iscariot, and doctors, like Luke, into his Father's business. He trained them in kingdom management skills, which included spiritual and natural laws, principles of productivity, responsibility, and accountability. These business partners were chosen according to his Father's will, meaning, as per the purposes for which they were born (Luke 6:12–13). Their previous occupations had prepared them to fulfill their divine assignment.

Carry on the Father's Business Legacy

Jesus had an educational program whereby he trained and mentored his disciples by example. This provided them with adequate knowledge and most importantly the skills to reign. He sent his disciples on hands-on-missions to practice the skills they had acquired. "After these things, the Lord appointed seventy others also, and sent them two by two before his face into every city and place where he himself was about to go" (Luke 10:1). And further instructed them, the would-be shepherds of his sheep, to depend on God as source of all resources.

As shepherds and custodians of the knowledge and skills of the kingdom restoration agenda, they had to depend solely on the Lord, the rightful owner of the sheep (Matthew 9:38) for their expenses, pay and reward, rather than bleeding the master's sheep for their livelihood. This was indeed the heart of their calling and a reminder that every divine vision has a divine provision. Therefore, anyone who crafts out an ambition rather than receiving a divine vision, will be on self-welfare. Employees depend on their employer for a paycheck and other benefits. Likewise, the disciples had been recruited by Jesus and had to rely on him for daily sustenance. Contrary to this, we see some so-called shepherds or men of God robbing the sheep, rather than feeding and tending to them (John 21:15).

Be Law-Abiding Citizens

During the earthly mission of Jesus, he demonstrated the returned government's power in diverse ways. This was geared toward ensuring that his followers witnessed and understood the principle of abiding with the law to access rights and privileges. Disobedience to the law disconnected man from his source and enabled the prince of darkness to hold them captive in perpetual cycles of sin. This is why Jesus said that setting the captives free was a divine directive as articulated in Luke 4:18: "To proclaim liberty to the captives."

He cautioned his followers to submit to all legal authority, most importantly to the Roman government under Pilate in Palestine at the time, and to pay all taxes. This was captured in his famous quote, "Render therefore to Caesar the things that are Caesar's, and to God the things that are God's" (Matthew 22:21). Paul writing to the Romans said, "Let every soul be subject to the governing authorities. For there is no authority except from God, and the authorities that exist are appointed by God" (Romans 13:1). This applies across all fields of life. Within marriages, the woman should submit to the man, who should be submitted to Christ, who is submitted to God (1 Corinthians 11:3). Likewise, in families, individuals should submit to the head of the family, within communities all members should submit to community leaders and in nations citizens should submit to all governing authorities (Romans 13:1-7; 1 Peter 2:13–14).

Jesus was exemplary when he submitted to his Father's will even to the death on the cross. His life was made a ransom to get the job done. Once the price was fully paid, mankind would receive grace to obey the laws of the home country and the devil would have no right to harass them because even though they are living on earth they would have another citizenship and constitution that they would submit to (Philippians 3:20). It is like an Asian with American citizenship being harassed by the American police on the streets of New York. Once the police officer realizes that the person in question is an American citizen, the battle line is redrawn. This is how Paul got himself out of a nasty whipping by the Roman soldiers when he declared he had Roman citizenship. He had dual nationality, Jewish and Roman (Acts 21:39; 22:29).

Believers who understand dual nationality know how to apply and enjoy their diplomatic immunity. Jesus was never intimidated by anything, whether it was a storm, or demon, or strong wind or pestilence. He knew he was from above and therefore above all (John 3:31; 19:11).

Respect and Obey the Constitution

The heart of all nations, empires and kingdoms is the constitution. In a kingdom, the constitution is the king's covenant with his citizens. It is initiated by the king and contains his aspirations and desires for his kingdom. The king's word is law and the constitution begins with "I, the Lord, say..." On the other hand, in democratic republics, the constitution is the covenant the people make with themselves and hire by vote a governing body to protect and keep it with them. It is the aspiration of the people and begins with the words "We, the people..."

The Bible is the constitution of the kingdom of heaven, the testament of the will of the king for his citizens. In a democracy we can change the constitution because we wrote it. But we cannot change God's constitution because we did not write it. This constitution from heaven to man contains the laws, rights, benefits, and privileges of the citizens. It is not affected by the environment, seasons, or conditions. The kingdom constitution possesses an unchanging standard against which all modern values, morals, beliefs, and ideas are measured. As with all constitutions, the penalties for violating them are prescribed.

The written laws for man to read and live by were not God's original intent. His intention was to write his laws on the hearts and minds of mankind so that no one would have to teach them. They were supposed to be customary and natural. Just imagine if we human beings were all law-abiding by nature, there would be no need for written laws, security systems and burglarproof premises. Our rebellion against God destroyed the rule of human conscience and made written law as well as human government necessary to protect society and restrain evil. Written law is intended to restore natural law to the conscience of mankind.

The written laws of God in the Scriptures have God's silent voice in the background, which can be referred to as the "Spirit of the law." It gives the reader understanding of the original meaning and purpose of the law. Laws are like keys that open locks. Problems arise when one does not know which key opens which lock. The same dilemma applies to some scholars and believers who quote scriptures out of context and expect hypothetical results. The Holy Spirit, who descended from heaven after the death, resurrection, and ascension of Jesus, is the only spirit that has the responsibility of teaching us how to identify and use these keys (John 14:26).

Uphold the Traits and Attitudes of Kingdom Citizenship

Jesus' message in Capernaum in the region of Galilee, called the Beatitudes, spelled out the right attitudes to have in the kingdom. "And seeing the multitudes, he went up on a mountain, and when he was seated his disciples came to him. Then he opened his mouth and taught them, saying, "Blessed are the poor in spirit, for theirs is the kingdom of heaven. Blessed are those who mourn, for they shall be comforted. Blessed are the meek, for they shall inherit the earth. Blessed are those who hunger and thirst for righteousness, for they shall be filled. Blessed are the merciful, for they shall obtain mercy. Blessed are the pure in heart, for they shall see God. Blessed are the peacemakers, for they shall be called sons of God. Blessed are those who are persecuted for righteousness' sake, for theirs is the kingdom of heaven" (Matthew 5:1–12).

The attitude ending with the phrase "for theirs is the kingdom of heaven" refers to citizenship and loyalty to the heavenly government which endows citizens with rights and privileges. This message laid the foundation for other messages that were delivered by Jesus during his "campaign trails" in synagogues, households, at water wells, along riverbanks and lake shores. Such a message can be highly effective in mobilizing others into the kingdom.

STRATEGIC DIRECTIONS TO RECLAIM THE COLONY

His method of delivering messages was unique. He spoke more in parables, which was intended to hide the truth until one was ready for it. He never wanted people to respond to what he said under duress or emotions, but rather with proper understanding and conviction. The messages, like capsules, were well confined and only released their contents in the appropriate medium.

Furthermore, a genuine thirst for the truth regarding kingdom principles, benefits and consequences were of essence in committing to the kingdom's lifestyle. This message motivated Rabbi Nicodemus, a Jewish religious leader, who for the first time understood the gospel of the kingdom that Jesus preached. The Rabbi opted to visit Jesus at night to find a way of entering the kingdom. Jesus answered and said to Nicodemus, "Most assuredly, I say to you, unless one is born of water and the Spirit, he cannot enter the kingdom of God" (John 3:5), meaning you have to believe the Word of God for the Holy Spirit to take up residence in you and make you a citizen of God's kingdom. Nicodemus desired citizenship of the kingdom of heaven and was shown the way into it. Jesus made him to understand that kingdom living required a change from religious ways of thinking to that of the kingdom, which is inspired by the Holy Spirit—received during the new birth.

Pay the Price

As the time for Jesus to pay the ultimate price for our deliverance and freedom with his own very life drew near, he cautioned that everyone that would follow him had to be ready to bear his or her own cross: "And whoever does not bear his cross and come after Me cannot be My disciple" (Luke 14:27). By this, he was referring to the commitment to him not only as Savior but also as Lord. The lordship principle is key when following Jesus. Accepting him as Lord is setting him above everything in your life, which is illustrated by the story of the rich young ruler.

This young man desired to become a citizen of the kingdom of heaven but was not ready to make the lordship commitment. He said to Jesus, "All these things (laws) I have kept from my youth. What do I still lack?" Jesus said to him, "If you want to be perfect, go, sell what you have and give to the poor, and you will have treasure in heaven; and come, follow Me." But when the young man heard that saying, he went away sorrowful, for he had great possessions" (Matthew 19:20–22).

He did not take into consideration the fact that all things belonged to God even his life, therefore, following the owner of everything meant he would own nothing but have everything. The kingdom of God does not tolerate conflict of interest and will not coax anyone to commit to its cause.

This is the reason why Jesus instructed kingdom citizens to put the heavenly business interest first. He said, "But lay up for yourselves treasures in heaven…" (Matthew 6:19–20). Every citizen prioritizes his home country. Partnering with God to build his kingdom on earth yields eternal reward. Being an excellent ambassador is not about sending wealth back to heaven, it is about being diligent in the resident country. That is, applying the policies and using all resources and strength to make the resident country look and function like the home country.

Deal with Conflict of Cultures

In colonization, there is a conflict of one culture with another because there is no room for co-existence but total infiltration that leads to the replacement of the lesser culture by the dominant one. The apostle Paul reiterated this by saying, "Therefore if anyone is in Christ, he is a new creation; old things have passed away; behold all things have become new" (2 Corinthians 5:17). There is no room for compromise. You are in or out, for him or against him (Revelation 3:15–16).

Religious people hated Jesus because he gave them no room to co-exist with their secret attitudes. Jesus reprimanded the religious rulers by saying, "Woe to you, scribes and Pharisees, hypocrites! For you shut up the kingdom of heaven against men; for you neither go in yourselves, nor do you allow those who are entering to go in" (Matthew 23:13).

The religious leaders understood that ignorance is a weapon of containment, so they hid knowledge from the poor masses. Many modern-day preachers do the same, like wolves in sheep clothing they maintain followers by preaching deliverance, prosperity, while mesmerizing them with arrays of "miracles" but hardly teach, train, mentor, and skill them into freedom. Jesus foreknew this and commissioned his assembly to make disciples and teach them to observe all things pertaining to the kingdom and its culture.

Changing people's ideology is the most difficult job on planet earth. Unfortunately, there are no quick fixes to cultural emancipation. It takes a wilderness experience and generations to deal with conflicting ideas, values and morals entrenched in people's subconsciousness. Cultural diversity if not properly understood can become the root cause of conflicts that transcends generations. In our current society we have people who want knowledge without character; pleasure without conscience; wealth without work; business without morality; politics without principles; and science without humanity.[15] Any effective change should embrace the culture of God's kingdom, which consists of righteous and just laws, and requires law-abiding citizenry.

Demonstrate Authority

Jesus healed, delivered, and fed the hungry to demonstrate the return of kingdom citizenship authority. This authority provided the desperately needed evidence regarding the working of the kingdom of God on the earth.

The pagan centurion, a Roman soldier under Caesar, whose servant Jesus healed displayed an understanding regarding the working of kingdom authority (Matthew 8:8). He understood kingdom principles and that caused Jesus to marvel at the faith he had, which was evidently lacking among the religious folks. Similarly, blind Bartimaeus had a revelation of the kingship of Jesus as son of David and asked for mercy (Mark 10:47). He got his miracle because he knew that only kings can have mercy. Kings do not need to consult anyone before taking a decision. A sharp contrast with presidents who would need a vote in parliament for a presidential pardon to be effected. The teaching style of Jesus and the miracles he performed were based on his authority as king.

Jesus cautioned the disciples against the pursuit of signs and wonders but emphasized that signs and wonders were to follow them as citizens of the kingdom because they carried heaven's governing authority. When the culture of heaven appears on earth, disorder becomes order (miracles) because the devil and his fallen angels tremble and flee from it. Jesus shocked the seventy disciples when they reported back to him, saying, "Lord, even the demons are subject to us in Your name" (Luke 10:17). He responded, "Nevertheless do not rejoice in this, that the spirits are subject to you, but rather rejoice because your names are written in heaven" (v. 20). He was reiterating kingdom citizenship authority above signs and wonders.

Handle Opposition the Kingdom Way

As David brought down Goliath to deliver the nation of Israel, so did Jesus come into the world to restore legitimate authority to all of humanity by bringing down satan. Handling opposition was an issue Jesus dealt with greatly when he walked the earth. Despite the opposition he encountered, he upheld the will of the father above his own and instructed his disciples to submit to God, resist the devil and he would flee (James 4:7).

Our responsibility is to understand that the battle against the devil was won more than two thousand years ago. We are then to approach any form of opposition with the mindset of victory. In the book of Acts, the apostles demonstrated the power of the restored kingdom authority by the miracles God performed through them. The battle had been won and authority restored. All that was and is required is faith in the victory Jesus accomplished on our behalf. He said, "These things I have spoken to you that you, that in Me you may have peace. In the world you will have tribulation; but be of good cheer, I have overcome the world" (John 16:33).

Jesus highlighted the importance of information in the battles of life by emphasizing knowledge of the truth, not just any knowledge, because one can have knowledge which is wrong. He said, "And you shall know the truth and the truth will make you free" (John 8:32). This was a new covenant version of Hosea 4:6, which states, "My people are destroyed for the lack of knowledge." The enemy will always insinuate, "If you are..." All he wants, is for you to believe a lie and doubt your self-identity in Jesus Christ, as God's righteousness. Once you doubt who and whose you are, fear creeps into your heart, wrong declarations are made, and the battle is lost. Adam failed this test in Eden and feared even the presence of God walking in the garden in the cool of the day (Genesis 3:8–11). Jesus, the second Adam, handled the opposition so beautifully by reminding the devil of what God had said about himself, mankind, and all other creation. In other words, Jesus declared what was written, therefore, until you know, believe, and declare what is written about you, you remain prey to satan who opposes anything godly.

When you believe in the victory of Jesus and what God says about you, you do not have to fight like Peter who took up a sword and chopped off the ear of a servant of the high priest. Jesus, having to redress the situation, said to him, "Put your sword in place, for all who take the sword will perish by the sword. Or do you think that I cannot now pray to My Father, and He will provide Me more than twelve legions of angels?" (Matthew 26:52–53). By implication, we are to handle opposition the kingdom way and yield to the counsel of the Holy Spirit who helps us to bear fruits of self-control and understanding just like Jesus.

As believers we have the governing authority of heaven, the Holy Spirit inside of us to help, comfort, guide, and counsel us on how to overcome opposition. For it is written, "You are of God, little children, and have overcome them, because He who is in you is greater than he who is in the world" (1 John 4:4).

Forge a Buy-In

Forging a buy-in into the kingdom concept was critical to ensure voluntary participation. Life is politics and God is the essence of life, there is therefore no distinction between government and spirituality. The assignment given to the first human (Adam), was a political assignment not a religious one. It is the same assignment that the second Adam (Jesus) came to fulfill, to reinstate the Creator's governing authority from heaven to earth, through a governing institution called the church.

Misunderstanding of the kingdom message gave rise to belief systems and religions that sort to alter the agenda of the church in the affairs of national governments. The church has a mandate from the King in heaven to influence all national governments to function as the governing authority in heaven. In that regard, the best form of government is a return to God's kingdom ideology. That is the acceptance to the call to sonship and divine inheritance (Galatians 4:6; Ephesians 1:11-14).

The buy-in into kingdom concepts by people in democracies or republics has been plagued by ignorance and the experience of corrupt kings and kingdoms in the past. This has made people to perceive kingdoms as dictatorships in the hands of families and caused the misunderstanding of Jesus and the recolonization agenda of the kingdom of heaven on the earth. Unlike other kingdoms, his kingdom is that of a benevolent king who cares for his citizens and his rule is a righteous one.

The heavenly king's benevolence, his love and compassion are the ingredients that attract both citizens and their governments to embrace the heavenly kingdom lifestyle on earth. The realization that we are sons with an inheritance, is vital to our kingdom walk. We are no longer servants but sons who work to expand our father's business. Therefore, the father's business is our business!

Personal Identification and Representation

You are citizens of the country of heaven, members of the royal family of God and ambassadors of Christ on the earth. Jesus never called his followers *Christians*. This was a demeaning label given by pagans to believers many years after Jesus had ascended into heaven (Acts 11:26). Jesus called his followers believers, ambassadors, citizens, kings, children and sons of God, God's workmanship, and friends.

The believer's identity is "an ambassador for Christ" by virtue of God's choice and representation. Jesus said, "You did not choose me, but I chose you and appointed you that you should go and bear fruits" (John 15:16). Ambassadors are chosen by the King and the government conferred upon them (Luke 22:29). They are guided in all truths by the knowledge of the constitution (John 16:13). As ambassadors, they have no personal opinion but that of the government (John 5:19). Members of parliaments, senators, mayors, counselors, etc. have to earn their position by canvassing for votes, whereas in a kingdom, conferring of the government upon ambassadors is a prerogative of the king.

Ambassadors reside on property owned by the home government and focus on the government's mandate and interest only. Once you have been chosen as an ambassador,

> ➤ you invent nothing but repeat policy from the home country;
> ➤ anyone who disagrees with the position of the policy of the government must take it up with the home country;

> your mode of operation is to understand the home country's position on every issue and restate it;
> your home country caters for you 100 percent;
> you do not have to fight, and have the understanding that civilians do not go to war because the army of the home country fights on their behalf;
> every crisis in the colony is an opportunity to display the glory of the home country's solutions;
> you own nothing, so cannot lose anything, with the paradox that all what the king owns is yours because he is your Lord (owner);
> you do not have to adopt the culture or traditions in the resident country but live according to the culture of your home country.

The ambassadors' authority comes from the same Holy Spirit that came upon the virgin and she conceived and bore a son. It is the same power that anointed Jesus of Nazareth to manifest the authority of the kingdom of heaven on earth and raised him from the dead. This same Spirit transforms believers and prepares them to function as ambassadors of the kingdom of heaven.

As appointed ambassadors, our assignment is already laid out for us, Jesus said, "I will build My church and the gates of Hades shall not prevail against it. And I will give you the keys of the kingdom of heaven" (Matthew 16:18–19). Which implies that until Jesus builds the church, anyone who builds will have it swallowed by hades, because they do not have the keys. Our message as his ambassadors, is to teach and preach the kingdom and its position on issues in our countries of residence. In the end, until the right message is taught and preached to the ends of the earth, the struggle continues.

Chapter 12

The Divine Announcement: Promise of the Governor's Return to the Colony

The goal of any kingdom is to make its colony function and look exactly like it. This is precisely what God purposed from the very beginning for the earth and its governing systems. He sent the Holy Spirit as governor to take on the responsibility of transforming the colony to the standards of the kingdom.

The Holy Spirit is the most eminent and excellent person in the colony, representing the presence of the absent king. His portfolio entails bringing the culture, values, nature, language, and lifestyle of the royal government to the colony and preparing the inhabitants for citizenship. A governor representing a king cannot live in an independent state, which is why the Holy Spirit was recalled when the colony declared independence.

After Jesus commissioned his "political party," he made an announcement about the return of the governor who left the colony when mankind declared independence saying, "But you shall receive power when the Holy Spirit has come upon you; and you shall be witnesses to Me in Jerusalem, and in all Judea and Samaria, and to the end of the earth" (Acts 1:8).

Aforetime to the fall of Adam and Eve, God breathed into them the Holy Spirit (Genesis 2:7)—the governor from heaven, who bestowed upon them the culture of the home country. This was to enable them embody the culture of heaven on earth, in thoughts, words and deeds.

At the declaration of independence, the governor was re-called and access to all home country rights and privileges withdrawn (Genesis 3:24). The colony became an orphan and had to develop its own governing systems. It was then that satan moved in as 'governor' and introduced a wicked government, called the kingdom of darkness. This government was illegal and had to be replaced.

Jesus came to deliver us from this kingdom and promised the return of the governor who would dismantle and replace the perverted kingdom's culture which had plunged the world systems into darkness, as it is written, "And I will pray the Father, and He will give you another Helper, that He may abide with you forever—the Spirit of truth, whom the world cannot receive, because it neither sees Him nor knows Him; but you know Him, for He dwells with you and will be in you. I will not leave you orphans; I will come to you" (John 14:16–18).

God delivered us from the power of darkness and conveyed us into the kingdom of the son of his love (Colossians 1:13). The severed relationship between the home country and colony had birthed perversion and given rise to diabolic governing systems. So, the announcement of the return of the governor was a wakeup call to freedom.

The death, resurrection, and ascension of Jesus into heaven would precede the return of the governor. The governor, who is the third person in the trinity, is a teacher, comforter, and counselor. His presence on earth would establish the assembly of believers called the church, which would be the governing agent that implements the mind of the king in the colony. His residence in the believers of Jesus would transform them to conform to the new governing systems. The governor's return would embody the presence of the absent King in the colony. Hence, the king does not need to be on earth while the governor is present, which justifies why King Jesus is in heaven at the right hand of the father (Ephesians 1:20).

Jesus never allowed his church to guess regarding the responsibilities of the governor, the Holy Spirit in the new dispensation. The Holy Spirit dwells only in believers who have been redeemed by the blood of the Lamb and is the only authorized teacher within each one of them. It is like a school where the teacher lives in the "students." The irony is that most "students" do not listen to what the teacher within is saying, but are more concerned with the "noise from without," like the music from the choir, theatrics of the preacher, entertainment, tithes and offerings and all sorts of emotional "sweet talks" and charisma. None of these aspects are wrong but the abusive use of them silence the Holy Spirit.

The function of the fivefold ministers, namely apostles, prophets, evangelists, pastors, and teachers, is to train or disciple believers to listen and obey the teacher within (Ephesians 4:11–12). What most of these ministers teach can be likened to "fish with bones," called sermons or doctrines. The teacher within has the responsibility to reveal and inspire the students to be able to sort out the "bones from the fish." In fact, most preachers give bony messages to the disciples and they swallow them wholesale. No wonder many believers end up as 'junk', full of empty words without corresponding lifestyles. They call Jesus Lord but do not submit to his lordship. Not surprising that Jesus questioned their motives for following him, when he said, "But why do you call Me Lord, Lord, and do not do the things which I say?" (Luke 6:46).

The Holy Spirit is the revealer of the truth and secrets of the keys of the kingdom of heaven. Unfortunately, some denominations and Bible scholars ignore the revealer of the truth of the message of the kingdom of God. They give heed to deceiving spirits, teach and preach doctrines of devils, as described by Paul in his letter to Timothy (1 Timothy 4:1–2). Many who follow such teachings have limited impact in the world's systems because they lack the revelation of the spirit of God.

The Holy Spirit, who is the spirit of truth has an impeccable résumé. He inspired 40 authors, over a period of approximately 1,500 years, to write the Scriptures, and the harmony of what they wrote is beyond human imagination. The Holy

Spirit is the sole author of the Bible, as it is written, "All Scripture is given by inspiration of God" (2 Timothy 3:16) and, "Knowing this first, that no prophecy of Scripture is of any private interpretation, for prophecy never came by the will of men, but holy men of God spoke as they were moved by the Holy Spirit" (2 Peter 1:20–21). In that regard, reading the Bible without the help of the author can be very dangerous, as it may lead to error, misinterpretation, out of context messages and people speaking to the Bible instead of the Bible speaking to them.

The governor does not speak on his own accord but on behalf of the home government. Ignore him at your own peril. His assignment is outlined by Jesus in John 16, "And when He has come, He will convict the world of sin, and of righteousness and of judgement: of sin because they do not believe in Me, of righteousness, because I go to my father and you see Me no more; of judgment because the ruler of this world is judged" (vv. 8–11). "However, when He the Spirit of Truth, has come, He will guide you into all truth; for He will not speak on his own authority, but whatever He hears He will speak and He will tell you things to come" (v. 13). In other words, the Holy Spirit is the administrator or custodian of the grace of God, to convict mankind to believe in the finished work of Jesus, who took away our iniquity, our disease and our poverty by becoming sin on our behalf, his body broken for our healing and his rejection for our acceptance, and the result of these events have put the ruler of this world under our feet.

Grace is unmerited favor; all that is required of humanity is to believe in the finished work of Jesus more than two thousand years ago at Calvary and be in tune with the counsel of the Holy Spirit, who transforms and replaces the old nature with the new one.

Chapter 13

The King on the Cross

The death of Jesus was a ransom to redeem the death penalty God had pronounced on humanity in the event that they disobeyed him. This was God's "Plan B" in case man rebelled against him. For this reason, it is written that, Jesus was the lamb slain from the foundation of the world (Revelation 13:8). Jesus himself declared that he laid down his life on his own accord: "Therefore My father loves Me, because I lay down My life that I may take it again. No one takes it from Me, but I lay it down Myself. I have power to lay it down, and I have power to take it again. This command I have received from My father" (John 10:17–18).

God had promised man that the day he disobeyed him and ate of the fruit he was instructed not to eat; he would surely die (Genesis 2:15–17). This was the first encounter man had with the concept of death. It existed but could not kill. Man's disobedience—rebellion against the known will of God, also called sin, gave life to death and allowed it to kill him. If Adam had not sinned, death would have remained dormant. God is faithful to his promise and protects his integrity. He had made provision to redeem man from the death penalty should they sin.

God took on a body to bear the death penalty pronounced on the man. His ultimate vision was to have a colony that would look and function like his kingdom. This purpose and vision for the colony and its systems have not changed. What changes are his plans to arrive at his destination.

God is trinity, meaning he is one but functions in three ways. He takes on many forms depending on who you know him to be. God like water can become ice and vapor. When he freezes, he becomes ice (the Word) and when he evaporates, he becomes vapor (the Holy Spirit). God personally revealed his true nature, his name, as I AM WHO I AM to Moses (Exodus 3:13–14). In that regard, God is whatever you know him to be in your life. As a rock he is the foundation on which you stand, as a spirit he exists and never dies, as a strong tower he has the best view of everything that happens. This should not be a surprise because he reveals himself to those who earnestly seek him (Proverbs 8:17).

The man Jesus was the body God needed to be legal and die to redeem man from the death penalty. God so loved the colony and his royal family that he had to give his Son, Jesus, to die to redeem the fallen human family and restore heaven's governing systems to the earth. Nonetheless, someone is always there to do the "dirty job" and fulfill prophecy. The part played by the Jewish religious leaders, Judas Iscariot, and the Roman soldiers which led to the crucifixion and death of Jesus were all intended to fulfill prophecy.

Forgiveness and reconciliation were made available to all of them. However, it is noted that only Peter who denied Jesus and the thief on the cross seized the opportunity. Scripture holds that both men were reconciled to the Lord. Jesus said to Peter a third time, "Simon son of Jonas, do you love Me?" And Peter said to Jesus, "Lord, You know all things; You know I love you." And Jesus said to him, "Feed My sheep" (John 21:17). Similarly, the thief on the cross said to Jesus, "Lord, remember me when You come into Your kingdom." And Jesus said to him, "Assuredly, I say to you, today you will be with Me in Paradise" (Luke 23:42–43).

Religion blinds people from accessing and accepting the truth. The Pharisees and Sadducees were no exception. They refused to see Jesus as the promised messiah who was to liberate the Jews from the oppressive colonial government, orchestrated by the Roman Empire. This rejection of the Messiah set the pace for the return of the heavenly government. The Jewish leaders wanted him dead! Therefore, they accused him before Pilate, saying, "We have a law, and according to our law he ought to die, because He made Himself the Son of God" (John 19:7). They perceived Jesus as a lunatic, hypocrite, demoniac, imposter and blasphemer and not the warring King they expected would lead the Jews to conquer the Roman occupation. They had no understanding of the role they and the Roman Empire were playing toward the fulfillment of prophecy concerning all that was written in the Old Testament about Jesus the Christ. Jesus, speaking to them, said, "O foolish ones, and slow of heart to believe in all that the prophets have spoken! Ought not the Christ to have suffered these things and to enter his glory? And beginning at Moses and all the Prophets, He expounded to them in all the scriptures the things concerning Himself" (Luke 24:25–27)

To this day, many Jews still wonder what the prophecy in Isaiah 53 is all about. Mind-boggling phrases such as, "He is despised and rejected by men, a Man of sorrows acquainted with grief"; "Yet we esteemed Him stricken, smitten by God and afflicted"; "And by His stripes we are healed"; "And the Lord laid on Him the iniquity of us all"; "Yet it pleased the Lord to bruise Him." Isaiah even went as far as saying, "He will be … a stone of stumbling and a rock of offense to both the houses of Israel, as a trap and a snare to the inhabitants of Jerusalem" (Isaiah 8:14). Such prophecies by a Jewish prophet must have caused confusion and even anger among his fellow countrymen.

The religious leaders could not find anything under the Jewish law to stone him to death for. When they brought him before the Sanhedrin Court with the high priest Caiaphas, Jesus remained silent because he was before a "wrong court-room": "And the high priest arose and said to Jesus, 'Do you answer nothing?' But Jesus kept silent" (Matthew 26:62–63). This infuriated them, so they accused him of treason before the Roman government. Consequently, he was referred by the high priest to Pilate, the Roman governor (John 19:12, 15), where they declared that they had only one king, Caesar, thus labelling Jesus a traitor, because he claimed to be king.

Jesus did not come to bring a religion but a government that is why he was not inclined to respond to the questions of the religious leaders. However, when he was taken before Pilate, he spoke because it was a government authority against another, the kingdom of Rome against the kingdom of heaven. Then Pilate entered the Praetorium again, called Jesus, and said to Him, "Are You the King of the Jews? Jesus answered him, are you speaking for yourself about this or did others tell you this concerning Me? Pilate answered, Am I a Jew? Your own nation and the chief priest have delivered You to me. What have You done? Jesus answered, My kingdom is not of this world. If My kingdom were of this world, My servants would fight, so that I should not be delivered to the Jews; but now My kingdom is not from here. Pilate said to Him, are you a king then? Jesus answered, you say rightly that I am king. For this cause I was born, and for this cause I have come into the world, that I should bear witness to the truth. Everyone who is of the truth hears My voice" (John 18:33–37).

The events in the Roman courtroom and those that followed were geared toward the fulfillment of the promise made thousands of years for the liberation of mankind from the shackles of the illegal governing system. God fervently waited thousands of years for the promise made in Eden, regarding the restoration of the kingdom of heaven to earth to be realized by Jesus. Human history had to take its course—the laws had been given and a right governing system was on the scene. The Jewish nation operated under the Law of Moses and the Roman Empire had an imperial law concept of citizenship with kings and lords. This is the implication of the prophetic writings that Jesus was born in the fullness of time, that reads, "But when the fullness of time had come, God sent forth His Son, born of a woman, born under the law" (Galatians 4:4).

Caesar, who was king in Rome had a governor called Pilate. He governed over the region of Judea and represented Caesar and his imperial law in the colony. Similarly, Jesus represented the kingdom of heaven on earth and interestingly his enemies recognized his kingdom message, but they did not want to submit to the authority of the heavenly government, so they sought to kill him. They told Pilate that Jesus was a threat to the political order of the day, saying, "We have no king but Caesar!" (John 19:15). They pressured Pilate by targeting his allegiance to Caesar and he caved in. Little did his enemies know that Jesus' death would lead up to his most important act on earth—the return of the governor from heaven.

Jesus was led to the cross as a man of sorrow, rejected, bruised, and afflicted. As a lamb, he did not fight back. He submitted to his Father's will. Even at the point of betrayal and arrest in the garden of Gethsemane where he had the choice to turn his back on the father's will, Jesus chose to obey him to the death (John 10:17–18). He said, "O My Father, if it is possible, let this cup pass from Me; nevertheless, not as I will but as You will." (Matthew 26:39). Though he had the power to summon legions of angels to fight for him, he chose to lay down his life (Matthew 26:53). While at the cross, when he was mocked, he said, "Father forgive them, for they do not know what they do" (Luke 23:34).

One of the thieves on the cross demonstrated that salvation was and remains a gift when he got his "passport" to paradise, not by works of the law but by grace. He believed and confessed Jesus as Lord. He said to Jesus, "Lord, remember me when You come into Your kingdom." And Jesus said to him, "Assuredly, I say to you, today you will be with Me in Paradise" (Luke 23:42–43).

"It is finished!" Those were the words echoed by Jesus before his death at the cross (John 19:30). This was in reference to his divine assignment, else he would have said, "I am finished." He had fulfilled the law and paid the price of sin that gave death the power to kill. The offense of disobedience and rebellion by Adam were deleted from the divine records, as foretold by prophet Isaiah, "I, even I, am He who blots out your transgressions for My Own sake; and I will not remember your sins" (Isaiah 43:25). And Paul echoed this new covenant deal in his epistle to the Hebrews, saying, "For I will be merciful to their unrighteousness, and their sins and their lawless deeds I will remember no more" (Hebrews 8:12).

After the death of Jesus, the father highly exalted him and gave him a name which is above every name, and "At the name of Jesus every knee should bow, of those in heaven, and of those on earth, and those under the earth" (Philippians 2:10). In that regard, those who believe in Jesus and the authority in his name, have been given the power of attorney to use it to overcome spiritual forces of darkness operating in the universe. The use of any other name is fake!

Works to appease, beg or cajole God to bless you are not more required. It is a done deal! We can now approach his throne with boldness, not crying and pity-parting. In this era, everything we do is to thank him for what he did more than two thousand years ago. We are once again restored as rightful heirs to implement his will on earth. Kingdom ambassadors do not beg or ask the king in the home country to come down and execute their God-ordained assignment, they simply get the job done. Ignoring your assignment as an ambassador and calling God to come down from heaven to deliver you or others is irresponsible. He has given you a mouth and wisdom to declare what you want done on earth (Luke 21:15). This confidence is referenced in the model prayer whereby the believer decrees, declares and then acts on the word of the king, so that what he said regarding a situation will come to pass.

The devil is under our feet (Romans 16:20). We are to stop bringing him up to the table of blessings, which was the case in the old covenant (Psalm 23:5). Refrain from calling on the Holy Spirit to come down, he is resident in you. Calling down fire from heaven to consume people is not right but manifesting the kingdom and getting people attracted to it, is. For the same reason, Jesus rejected the request made by James and John to allow them command fire from heaven to consume the Samaritans who had rejected him; he turned and rebuked them saying, "You do not know what manner of spirit you are of. For the Son of Man did not come to destroy men's lives but to save them" (Luke 9:54–55).

We are to tame our tongues; quit using empty words and walk the talk. Stop crying to God as Moses did instead of using the power in the rod given to him to open the Red Sea (Exodus 14:15–16). Declare the New Testament "rod," the word of the Lord as it is written, and the devil will flee. Discontinue seeking the old covenant power of Elijah and the wisdom of Solomon. Jesus said that greater than they is here and we are expected to look only unto him, the only mediator between God and man, the author and finisher of our faith. He alone is the fulfillment of prophecy, the ultimate power and wisdom of God. He reminds the believer that the Holy Spirit that came upon Elijah and Solomon has taken aboard in us and made us even greater that John the Baptist who came in the spirit of Elijah. He said, "Assuredly, I say to you, among those born of women there has not risen one greater that John the Baptist, but he who is least in the kingdom is greater than he" (Matthew 11:11). John was greater than all the prophets because he had "one leg" in the Old Testament and the other in the new, meaning he did not only prophesy about Jesus, he saw and introduced him to his ministry (Matthew 3).

If the believer is greater than John, by implication he or she is greater than Moses, Elijah, Jeremiah, etc. These great men of faith died only having received the promise of the coming King, but we have beheld his glory. The Holy Spirit that could not live in them now dwells in us who have been washed by the blood of the Lamb. We should move from deliverance-only ministries to setting the captives free, by teaching the truth that transforms the mind.

The expression, "It is finished" destroyed the reign of the devil and heaven rejoiced because the legitimate government was finally in the hands of the rightful heirs. The "heavenly kingdom flag" was once again raised in the colony while the "human independence flag" was simultaneously being lowered. This signaled the reconciliation of humanity with the king and his kingdom. The divine mandate to govern and dominate the earth and to make it look like heaven was back. God's royal family was once again in charge.

Chapter 14

The Resurrection of the King

The devil nailed Jesus to the cross while Christ killed the devil. Ponder on this statement for a while. It is not a religious statement but a kingdom revelation. True to what God had promised the serpent in the garden, the Seed of the woman would bruise his head and he would bruise the Seed's heel (Genesis 3:15). Authority is in the head and that was exactly what Jesus, the Seed of the woman crushed. This was foreshadowed in the Old Testament, wherein it was narrated that David went straight for Goliath's head (1 Samuel 17:49, 51).

In the fullness of time, the Word of God became flesh and dwelt among us in the form of a man, Jesus (John 1:1, 14). His anointed Word (Christ) was conceived in a body that was formed in the womb of a virgin by the Holy Spirit. Jesus often referred to himself as Son of Man and Son of God. That is the Christ, the Son of God, concealed in the body of Jesus the Son of Man that was revealed to Peter when he confessed Jesus, not as the son of Joseph but as Christ, the son of the living God (Matthew 16:16). It is the Son of Man who died and was raised up by Christ, the Son of God.

When Jesus died, Christ left his body and descended into Hades to set the captives free (Ephesians 4:8–9; Acts 2:29–39). The captives were Old Testament saints who had died before the death of Jesus and their souls went to Sheol or Hades (Psalm 16:10). In retrospect, after the rebellion of Adam, man became unrighteous to stand before God, so all those that died in faith went to Hades or Abraham's bosom (Luke 16:22) waiting for the redemptive blood of the Lamb of God to be shed (Hebrews 9:22). In Hades, one can only imagine that Christ needed an alibi to testify that Jesus truly died to pay the price of sin and his dead body lay in the tomb. Being that one cannot testify of themselves; he would need an eyewitness to close the case against satan and his reason for holding men captive claiming that man legally handed over their authority to him by disobeying God. To the devil's disappointment, Christ had a witness (the redeemed thief on the cross) in paradise (Luke 23:43) to testify to the death of Jesus whose blood had been shed for the remission of sin. The body of the Lamb of God paid that price and closed the case when he said, "It is finished!"

Christ seized the keys of life and death from satan and made a public spectacle of him when he exposed him for who he really was and is—an imposter (Colossians 2:15; 2 Corinthians 11:14). He opened the doors of Hades and raised up the dead and people witnessed the graves giving way to living bodies, as it is written, "And the graves opened; and many bodies of the saints who had fallen asleep were raised; and coming out of the graves after His resurrection, they went into the holy city and appeared to many. So, when the centurion and those who saw him, who were guarding Jesus, saw the earthquake and the things that had happened, they feared greatly, saying, Truly this was the Son of God!" (Matthew 27:52–54).

On the third day Christ returned from Hades victorious and raised Jesus from the dead, given that his body knew no corruption—without sin (Acts 2:31). Christ needed this body to continue his post resurrection operations on earth. And the 40 days post resurrection on earth before ascending into heaven were filled with drama.

Jesus the Christ, had to diffuse the forgery and corruption of the religious folks, who had bribed the soldiers, the first witnesses of the resurrection to lie against his disciples saying that they had stolen his body while they slept. Accounts of these felonies are recorded in the book of Matthew, saying, "Behold some of the guard came into the city and reported to the chief priests all the things that had happened. When they had assembled with the elders and consulted together, they gave a large sum of money to the soldiers, saying, tell them, His disciples came at night and stole Him away while we slept. And if this comes to the governor's ears, we will appease him and make you secure. So, they took the money and did as they were instructed; and this saying is commonly reported among the Jews until this day" (Matthew 28:11–15).

To silence the rumors, like many political fixers, the elders had to give the soldiers huge sums of money and they had no choice but to accept the payoff because under the Roman law, it was a treasonable act for a soldier to sleep on duty. Secondly, if the elders had not bribed them to tell the lie, everyone would have believed their story given that they had no personal interest in the matter. God is smart, he made sure the soldiers witnessed the resurrection before his disciples, since the disciples had a personal interest in the matter and people would doubt their version. Religious folks have not changed since then. They can pay anyone to compromise the message of the kingdom, purpose of the cross, death, and resurrection of Jesus the Christ.

After the resurrection, Jesus appeared to the disciples and recalled them into his Father's business. He also appeared to two of his disciples on the road to Emmaus and testified that all the Old Testament scriptures were about him (Luke 24:13–35). Knowing that many had lost hope and returned to their previous occupations, notably Peter, who had gone back to fishing, Jesus understood their predicament and restored them to their original assignment. He then breathed upon them the same breath God had breathed into the first couple before the fall in Eden (John 20:22; Genesis 2:7). Thereafter, he continued to preach the message of the kingdom of heaven on earth and verified if the message he had proclaimed was the same that his disciples were teaching and preaching.

The death of Jesus and resurrection were in line with God's Word and fulfilled the laws and prophecies. It was not an option, the time for redemption had arrived. No amount of animal sacrifices as was the pattern introduced in the Old Testament, could ever atone for the sin of man. Only the blood of the Lamb of God could. The resurrection was a demonstration that even when we die physically, we will rise to govern the colony with Jesus once again.

Chapter 15

The King Ascends into Heaven and the Governor Returns to the Colony

Forty days after the resurrection, Jesus gathered his disciples and announced his departure to heaven. Hitherto, he had communicated his ascension to Mary Magdalene who met him after his resurrection. Jesus revealed himself to her as the resurrected Lord and instructed her to communicate the resurrection to the disciples. He said to her, "Do not cling to me, for I have not yet ascended to my Father; but go to my brethren and say to them, I am ascending to My Father and Your Father, and to My God and your God" (John 20:17).

The drama before the ascension was well documented by Luke the apostle, in the book of Acts where he highlighted the announcement concerning the return of the governor, the Holy Spirit from heaven to earth, "And being assembled together with them, He commanded them not to depart from Jerusalem, but to wait for the Promise of the Father" (Acts 1:4).

While the disciples watched, Jesus was taken up, and a cloud received him out of their sight (v. 9).

Jesus died and was raised up by Christ, who first descended into Hades and raised to life the saints that died before the shading of the blood of the Lamb of God. The same Christ who raised the body of Jesus from the dead, took Jesus to heaven and put him at the right hand of the Father. This fulfilled what King David prophesied about the Lord Jesus saying, "The Lord said to My Lord, sit at My right hand till I make Your enemies Your footstool (Psalm 110:1).

The divine strategic plan was that Christ who lived in Jesus would take Jesus into heaven and then return into another body, the assembly of the saints of God, who are also called the church. This explains why the church is referred to as the body of Christ, not Jesus (1 Corinthians 12:27). Therefore, anyone convicted of sin by the Holy Spirit, repents and confesses Jesus' death and resurrection receives Christ, the eternal Word of God.

The confession of faith is the first step in the journey of salvation. Transformation of the mind is the next step. The Holy Spirit that convicts you into salvation continues to reveal to your mind the Word of God, in order to transform your mind to conform to that of Christ. Scripture has it that we are not to be conformed to this world, but be transformed by the renewing of our minds (Romans 12:2), even as it is written, "Let this mind be in you which was also in Christ Jesus" (Philippians 2:5).

The death of Jesus, his resurrection and ascension into heaven ushered the return of the Holy Spirit to planet earth to complete God's strategic plan of restoring his glory back to the colony. The redemption plan for his royal family to oversee the colony was virtually a done deal.

The plan, which can be referred to as our redemption package, comprises of three components, two of which have been successfully delivered, namely, the salvation of the spirit and transformation of the soul. The third component, which is the resurrection of the body is yet to take place. However, one has to be fully aware that the first two components are continuous processes as long as the Holy Spirit who dwells in the church remains on earth (2 Thessalonians 2:6–7; John 12:32).

The human being is spirit, soul, and body (1 Thessalonians 5:23) and the redemption package liberates the tripartite person as follows:

I. The redemption of the spirit is a free gift, as we confess with our mouths the Lordship of Jesus and believe in our hearts that God raised him from the dead (Romans 10:9).

II. The redemption of our soul (mind, will and emotions) is the renewing and transformation of our mindset. It is a choice we make, to partner with the Holy Spirit that we receive at salvation, to hear, read, study, and meditate on the Word of. God. We work out the salvation of our soul with fear and trembling, and not by conforming to worldly thought patterns and lifestyles (Philippians 2:12). It is by the authority of the Holy Spirit in us and the truth we know that gives credibility to our freedom to walk in dominion on the earth (John 8:32).

III. The redemption of our bodies (Romans 8:23) is also a free gift by God through the resurrection power of Jesus Christ at his second coming, as it is written, "For the Lord Himself will descend from heaven with a shout, with the voice of an archangel, and with the trumpet of God. And the dead in Christ shall arise first. Then we who are alive and remain shall be caught up together with them in the clouds to meet the Lord in the air" (1 Thessalonians 4:16–17).

Having the mind of Christ is living in the consciousness that the "change agent" of mental transformation—the Holy Spirit, who dwells in you, is the key to dominion. He is the master revealer of the secret keys of the kingdom of heaven and our guide into all truths. Jesus promised that his ascension into heaven would enable the father to send the Holy Spirit back to earth—a promise that was fulfilled at Pentecost.

The Holy Spirit convicts us of sin and righteousness through Christ, the Word of God. He guides us into the understanding that even though we are on earth, our citizenship is in heaven and we have been raised and made to sit together in heavenly places far above all principality, power, might, dominion and every name that is named, not only in this age but also in that which is to come (Ephesians 1:20–21; 2:6). He reminds us of every spiritual blessing the father has blessed us with in heavenly places in Christ (Ephesians 1:3). Therefore, heaven is the source of all the resources we require to reign on earth and discharge our earthly mandate.

The ascension of Jesus into heaven, the return of the Holy Spirit and the open-door policy between heaven and earth established a commonwealth of citizens called the church, not a religious group. This portal between the heaven and the earth and the commissioning of the church were foreshadowed in the Old Testament by the dream Jacob had of a ladder set up on the earth reaching heaven with angels of God ascending and descending on it (Genesis 28:10–22). In this dream God promised to spread Jacob's seed all over the earth through which all the families of the earth would be blessed. Jacob fully aware of what he had just experienced said, "How awesome is this place! This is none other than the house of God, and this is the gate of heaven!" (v. 17).

The open-door policy gives us audience with God and guarantees resources for us to utilize and make the colony function just like the home country. Provision of resources from the headquarters to the colony is God's kingdom commonwealth principle. This is a direct opposite with the kingdoms of the world that extract from their colonies. Unlike the world systems, whereby one needs to book an appointment, have to pass through several checks and security gates to see the king, in the kingdom of heaven, the king leaves his throne and comes to the gate, opens it and says whosoever will come in, will sit with me on the throne in heavenly places (Ephesians 2:6).

Jesus did not leave us without a connection to our home country when he ascended into heaven. As our great high priest in heaven, Jesus sent the Holy Spirit to counsel us that we may approach the throne of grace with boldness and obtain mercy and find grace to help us execute our divine assignment on the earth (Hebrews 4:14–16).

Chapter 16

The Great Commission

The Great Commission is the 'common mission' given to the body of Christ to galvanize humanity into the grand finale—the invasion of the world's systems by the government of heaven. It communicates God's mandate to the church, the constituent assembly of God on earth. It reiterates God's plan to restore or see his eternal purpose for the world and earth fulfilled, through his royal family.

The commission is a means to an end, not an end in itself. As a means, it is a mission. But the end is the alignment of the mission to the vision, which is the government of heaven on earth. Jesus speaking to his disciples said, "All authority has been given to Me in heaven and on earth. Go therefore and make disciples of all the nations, baptizing them in the name of the Father and the Son and the Holy Spirit, teaching them to observe all things that I have commanded you, and lo, I am with you always, even to the end of the age" (Matthew 28:18–20).

The Great Commission flagged off by Jesus set the pace for the great contest between the two "opposing parties," the kingdom of light and that of darkness, seeking for the very heart of man and the governing systems on earth.

Sometimes one wonders if the church is aware of these events or if it fully grasps the role it plays as ambassadors to the world and high commissioners to the commonwealth assembly of believers. It appears the church has ignored the purpose for which the commission was established, which is to dominate and subdue the earth with the culture of heaven (Genesis 1:26; Matthew 6:10). Instead of making disciples, it has focused on making converts, who are left to their own devices, thereby preoccupying themselves with leaving the earth than mastering it. The Great Commission assignment was intended for the church to teach and mold disciples into true ambassadors of the heavenly government who can bring the culture of the home country to impact the earth.

Making converts rather than disciples has been the undoing of the church. The world scorns the church because it does not have the corresponding lifestyle to that of Christ. The church puts emphasis on making converts who are not properly equipped and therefore seek benefits or entitlements, without taking full responsibility. They love Jesus as Savior but not as Lord. As Savior because they enjoy the free gift of forgiveness and "fire insurance," but they do not want him as Lord, because lordship requires obedience to him. The church is yet to make the sons of light as shrewd as the sons of the world, who understand and apply the concepts of stewardship, planning, diligence, consistency and perseverance to prosper on earth (Luke 16:8).

The focus of the church has become the celebration of what Jesus did, rather than what he did it for. We worship Calvary and the ideas of going to heaven instead of accepting the promise to dominate the earth. We have made the process the purpose, while abdicating our roles as representatives of Christ on the earth.

Without adequate training and modeling, some believers continue to be at the bottom of the "food chain," singing "I'll Fly Away"[16] and "I Got Shoes."[17] When one observes these traits in Christendom, they could be tempted to say the church has misrepresented the King, his kingdom and his message of restoring the kingdom government on earth.

As stakeholders in this commission, we have the responsibility to heed the guidance of the Holy Spirit, obey and acknowledge the authority of Jesus over all spheres of our lives. In so doing, we will govern the earth and make it look like the home country.

We are diplomats, and as ambassadors we carry the glory of the country of heaven on the earth. We have been commissioned by Jesus to show the world how the kingdom of heaven functions. On that account, we should be like him to the extent that unbelievers see his nature in us, and the ruler of this world's fallen systems would have nothing of his in us (John 14:30).

We are to guard our hearts from corruption and choose our words carefully, never exploding in anger and staying away from inappropriate places, because whatever the ambassador does, the global community will impute to the country being represented. Jesus, representing his Father on earth, said, "He who has seen Me has seen the Father" (John 14:9). The question is, when the world sees you, who do they see?

Chapter 17

The Birth of the Assembly of Christ—The Church at Pentecost

The event in the upper room in Jerusalem marked the return of the governor to the colony. Before ascending into heaven, Jesus told the disciples to wait for the Promise of the Father, the Holy Spirit, also known as the Governor to the Colony.

It was rather unfortunate that even the disciples at that moment had not fully grasped the true essence of the kingdom message and were still asking for a Jewish kingdom. They asked Jesus, "Lord, will You at this time restore the kingdom to Israel? (Acts 1:6). And he responded, "But you shall receive power when the Holy Spirit has come upon you; and you will be witnesses to Me in Jerusalem, and in all Judea and Samaria, and to the end of the earth" (v. 8). Jesus was talking about a global kingdom—a world conquest, whereas the disciples were thinking of a national government.

Many denominations, prophesying Christ, have not known any better. They are focused on their ethnic groups and religious sects or constituencies rather than being witnesses, ambassadors or representatives of the government Jesus brought to the entire world. Jesus understood the challenge of his disciples and promised them that the governor from heaven would be sent to empower and transform their minds to think and act as citizens of heaven on earth.

The return of the Holy Spirit would transform the world systems and its inhabitants into the original king's ideal colony. The day of Pentecost—like D-Day, was when the church, the assembly of Christ, was born as an agent of change in the colony to empower the followers of Jesus to preach and teach the gospel of the kingdom and extend its influence by making other disciples. The disciples would bring the original heavenly kingdom model back to planet earth, by building kingdom minded individuals, families, communities, and nations.

It is written, "When the Day of Pentecost had fully come, and they were all in one accord in one place. And suddenly there came a sound from heaven, as a rushing mighty wind, and it filled the whole house where they were sitting. Then they appeared to them divided tongues, as of fire, and one sat upon each of them. And they were filled with the Holy Spirit and began to speak with other tongues, as the Spirit gave them utterance" (Acts 2:1–4).

The bottom line is that they were empowered by the governor from heaven, and Peter, who had once denied Jesus, was so emboldened that he preached a sermon that caused three thousand souls to become ambassadors for Christ (Acts 2:41). It is amazing to see the contrast between the law of Moses in the old dispensation and the law of righteousness in the new dispensation. The law of Moses was a pacesetter for the law of righteousness by Jesus. When Moses, the foreshadow of Jesus, brought down the Ten Commandments written on tablets of stone, three thousand people fell (Exodus 32:28), but when Jesus sent down the Holy Spirit to write the law of righteousness in the hearts of men, three thousand souls were saved (Acts 2:41). This testifies to the scriptures that say, "Christ is the end of the law for righteousness to everyone who believes" (Romans 10:4), and "for the law of the Spirit of life in Christ Jesus has made me free from the law of sin and death" (Romans 8:2).

The Holy Spirit convicts of sin and draws the sinner to Christ. Once you believe, the law of the right nature of God is written in your heart. Therefore, the importance of the return of the Holy Spirit at Pentecost cannot be overemphasized. For the church to be effective in expanding the kingdom's influence throughout the earth, it must acknowledge and embrace the counsel and guidance of the Holy Spirit. In so doing, the church will rise to its mandate and give the devil and his fallen angels, hell on earth.

The government of heaven has returned, and the battle has been won. So, walking in victory and extending the influence of the kingdom of heaven on earth is the church's primary responsibility.

Chapter 18

The Ambassador's Portfolio and Message

We have come a long way in our journey to unravel the mysteries of creation, its purpose and the role mankind plays in its existence. Our efforts to understand the divine agenda and program to recolonize the earth and restore man's lost glory in ruling over creation have provided information of the truth, our origin, destination and offered some answers to many of our questions.

Throughout our journey into the mind of the Creator, we have found that our origin is in him, and we are created in his image and likeness (Genesis 1:26). As is the case for any manufacturer, the intended destination for the product made is to take total control of the marketplace. This explains why God created and commissioned us to earth: so, we can manifest his glory and dominate in all areas of gifting (John 17:22; Matthew 6:10).

This destination was intentional because God wanted to expand his kingdom from the unseen to the seen realm and provide his offspring with a different territory from his own to exercise sovereignty. Heaven therefore is not our final destination, as we are taught in most of our church lessons, but an assembly point from which we will return with Jesus to the earth to rule forever (Revelation 5:10, John 17:15). So, preoccupation with the thoughts of returning to the manufacturing plant are not right because they disrupt and hinder the manufacturer's purpose for creation. All manufacturers build, test, ok and sign off their products. In like manner, God equipped mankind to take control of the systems of the world and impact them with the culture of the kingdom of heaven.

However, this can only be done if we fully understand our roles and the message we are to communicate as we go about our assignment to ensure that the heavenly culture impacts the earth. Jesus effectively communicated his end time message after narrating the events that would precede his return. "And this gospel of the kingdom will be preached in all the world as a witness to all nations, and then the end will come" (Matthew 24:14). This message was encapsulated in his first public pronouncement concerning his mission on earth: "The kingdom of heaven has returned" (Matthew 4:17). His mission statement and his end time message were centered on God's eternal program to extend his kingdom from the unseen to the seen realms for his family to have sovereign rule (Genesis 1:26).

Our God is awesome! His ways of communication beat our imagination. Truly there is none like him, declaring the end from the beginning, and from ancient times things that are not yet done (Isaiah 46:9–10). He revealed his kingdom restoration agenda in the beginning to Abraham, saying, "In you all families of the earth shall be blessed" (Genesis 12:3). He later restated the same promise to Jacob, whose name was changed to Israel, the natural seed of Abraham, stating, "I am the Lord God of Abraham your father and the God of Isaac; the land on which you lie I will give to you and your descendants. And your descendants shall be like the dusts of the earth; you shall spread abroad to the west and to the east, to the north and to the south; and in you and in your seed all the families of the earth shall be blessed" (Genesis 28:13–14).

This promise was later fulfilled through Jesus, the Word of God, the spiritual Seed of Abraham, in whom God reconciled the Jews and Gentiles (Ephesians 2:11–22). Jesus reiterated the Promise of the Father to the disciples, who would champion the New Testament congregation of Jews and Gentiles, the church, when He said, "But you shall receive power when the Holy Spirit has come upon you; and you shall be witnesses to me in Jerusalem, and in all Judea and Samaria, and in to the ends of the earth" (Acts 1:8).

The church, made of Jews and Gentiles, cannot fail. It has the responsibility to understand, communicate and apply the will of the father to all humanity. Effective communication of the constitution to the citizens is paramount in all kingdoms and national governments. It is both an art and a science that the body of Christ needs to study and apply. Satan, the prince of the power of the air, understood the relevance and power of airwaves in communication, which explains why he took his abode in the air (Ephesians 2:2). It is essential that as ambassadors we understand the power in the airwaves and use them to the advantage of the expansion of the kingdom's agenda.

For the body of Christ to effectively control the narrative, we should counteract the diabolic ideologies broadcasted through the airwaves by establishing robust departments of communication within the ministries. The ministry of communication is next to that of defense. In the event of a coup, the perpetrators work tirelessly to control the media houses. Bible history states the existence of such ministries and their appropriate leadership. The archangel Michael is in charge of defense while Gabriel heads communication. Michael led the army of God to defeat and overthrow satan out of heaven (Revelation 12:7) while Gabriel communicated the birth of the Son of God (Luke 1:26–28), who would crush the head of the serpent—a job well done by the two ministries, leaving the enemy neutralized above and below and the baton handed over to the sons of God.

The heavens now declare the updated weapons of our warfare, thus, "they overcame him by the blood of the Lamb and by the word of their testimony" (Revelation 12:11). If you fight with earthly weapons and methods, you are meat for the enemy because that is his arena and he is full of wrath against the inhabitants of the earth. So, take up citizenship in heaven and put on the righteousness of Jesus, then his blood and your testimony of his lordship over your life brings satan and his demons under your feet.[18]

Under the lordship of Jesus, believers become representatives of the government of heaven on earth. In our ambassadorial capacity, we are fully equipped to communicate the correct, uncensored message of the king to the ends of the earth. However, to effectively communicate this assignment, we must first understand and apply the truth regarding our repositioning as citizens of the kingdom of heaven seated far above all principalities and powers controlling the territories in which we live.

The prince of the power of the air, the ruler of this world, was disarmed and has no authority over those who understand that though they are in this world, their citizenship is in heaven far above all principalities and powers (Colossians 2:15; Ephesians 2:6). The devil has territorial control only over those under his jurisdiction, who have not taken up heavenly citizenship, or those who are ignorant of their new citizenship status. His strategies are aimed at blinding unbelievers from taking up kingdom citizenship and causing those that have taken up citizenship to walk in unrighteousness and as a result lose their kingdom benefits (2 Corinthians 4:3–4).

As citizens of heaven, we should perceive challenges in the world as opportunities to manifest our home country's authority and expand its influence. We need to stand still and boldly speak to any situation, as Jesus did when he stood before Pilate who was the earthly governing authority over Palestine and declared, "You could have no power at all against Me unless it was given to you from above" (John 19:11). Authority such as this starts by first fully understanding and communicating the right message of the kingdom of heaven's return to the earth.

PART II

COMMUNICATING
THE KING'S
MESSAGE

Chapter 19

The Gospel of the Kingdom

The theme that runs throughout the teachings and miracles of Jesus is identified in his opening statement in Matthew 4:17: "The kingdom of heaven is at hand." This opening statement was the pronouncement of the return of the heavenly governing authority that departed from the colony of earth when mankind committed treason and severed themselves from the home country.

Jesus at multiple occasions, reiterated the phrase, "The kingdom of heaven is like..." And the gospel of Matthew captures many of these phrases, such as, "The Kingdom of heaven is like a man who sowed good seeds in his field, but while men slept, his enemy came and sowed tares among the wheat and went his way (13:24–25). "Again the kingdom of heaven is like treasure hidden in the field, which a man found and hid it and for the joy over it he goes and sells all that he has and buys that field" (v. 44). And again, "The kingdom of heaven is like a merchant seeking beautiful pearls, who, when he had found one of great price, went and sold all that he had and bought it" (vv. 45–46).

Jesus centered all his messages on the return of the kingdom of heaven to earth. He told the crowd in Galilee, "I must preach the kingdom of God to the other cities also, because for this purpose I have been sent" (Luke 4:43). The message of the return of the kingdom of heaven to earth is the purpose for which Jesus came. He came with the kingdom government upon his shoulder (Isaiah 9:6) and as is the case with all kingdoms, the king and his message were heralded by a forerunner or messenger. John the Baptist was sent as the messenger to announce the king and his message. It is written, "In those days John the Baptist came preaching in the wilderness of Judea, and saying, "Repent, for the kingdom of Heaven is at hand!" For this is he who was spoken of by Prophet Isaiah, saying: "The Voice of one crying in the wilderness: 'Prepare the way of the Lord; make His paths straight" (Matthew 3:1–3).

In the days of John and Jesus, every master teacher or rabbi had a school of thought with a unique message and method of initiating students into the school. At age thirty any student had the option of opening his own school of thought or submitting to one. John turned thirty, six months ahead of Jesus his cousin and opened his school based on the message of the kingdom and moved into the wilderness, baptizing his followers in water. He baptized with water for repentance but promised the coming of one after him who would baptize with the Holy Spirit (Matthew 3:11–12).

Jesus identified and submitted to John's school of thought and was baptized, as it is written, "And John tried to prevent Him, saying, 'I need to be baptized by you and you are coming to me?' But Jesus answered and said to him, 'Permit it to be so now, for thus it is fitting for us to fulfill all righteousness" (Matthew 3:14–15); and "from that time Jesus began to preach and to say, 'Repent, for the kingdom of heaven is at hand" (4:17).

The forerunner—John the Baptist, and the king Jesus both carried the same message of the good news of the return of the heavenly governing authority to the earth.

Jesus, at age thirty, while referring to John, said he was the greatest prophet to be born of a woman (Matthew 11:11). John prophesied about the Messiah, saw him, announced his message, then ushered and signed him into his ministry by baptism. Baptism by water was John's sign of initiating one into his school of thought. In that regard, one had to fully understand and commit to the unique message of the master teacher before taking the sign of initiation.

Today, many of us get baptized without fully understanding the message of the kingdom. This is the very message that God gave to John, which Jesus submitted to, preached, taught, and then instructed his disciples to do the same. For instance, Philip a disciple of Jesus, had to explain the meaning of what the prophet Isaiah had prophesied concerning Jesus and based on that understanding, the Ethiopian Eunuch was baptized as a sign of his belief in Christ (Acts 8:26–39). Similarly, Peter commanded Cornelius and his household to be baptized after they understood the message of the kingdom and received the

Holy Spirit (Acts 10:34–47). Therefore, taking a sign without understanding it's purpose, is likened to a dry sinner who is immersed into water and comes out as a wet sinner.

Baptism simply confirms your acceptance, belief, understanding and commitment to the kingdom school of thought, "The return of the kingdom of heaven." Once you believe in the death, burial, and resurrection of Jesus you are saved. Immersion into water then serves as an endorsement to the message Jesus preached and your commitment to become his ambassador and convey the same message to all the world (Matthew 28:19–20). Thereafter, understanding and applying the right kingdom message to all spheres of life is crucial to all ambassadors who desire to impact the world for the kingdom they represent.

The message of the gospel of the kingdom is about the good news of God restoring man's lost dominion over the earth. It is God's master plan to return the kingdom governing authority to the sons who inhabit the colony—earth. The kingdom message is the reason for all the laws, prophets and the purpose for which Jesus was sent. It is also the core message in the Bible and a shared sentiment in this book about a King who sent his Son from his kingdom into the colony to recapture power from an illegally established government and return the governing authority to its rightful heirs—mankind. This implies that any message contrary to the return and establishment of the kingdom of heaven to the earth is out of order and bound to fail.

Humans are searching for what they lost—delegated authority to dominate the earth and its governing systems. The message of the returned kingdom of heaven to the earth confers upon us our original citizenship that was lost, and the kingdom power to rule, dominate and make the earth function like heaven. Until we fully embrace this message and walk in it, there would be no rest for our souls, regardless of whatever we do or possess.

While on earth we enjoy dual nationality, divine and natural. With our divine citizenship, we represent the government of heaven on earth and enjoy diplomatic immunity. On the other hand, our natural citizenship makes us legal on earth to manifest the culture of the country of heaven on earth. This message about the recovery of our heavenly citizenship and earthly rulership was what John introduced and Jesus preached, and everyone was rushing into it (Luke 16:16). It was not about leaving earth for heaven but governing the earth and making it function like heaven.

Jesus made reference to his birth, his death and even his resurrection as a means to return to the rightful heirs of the earth and its systems, the dominion mandate they lost. The preaching of the law and prophets was until John the Baptist (Luke 16:16). He initiated the preaching of the kingdom of heaven, then Jesus fulfilled and commissioned it to be preached to the ends of the world (Matthew 3:2; 24:14). Jesus taught principles of the kingdom wrapped in parables and made an Old Testament background check. But often, we do the reverse by preaching Old Testament stories and then sugar coating them with some wooden cross messages in his name. The principle of the kingdom message is about taking up kingdom citizenship and manifesting heaven's culture on the earth, and not abnegating responsibility and blaming it on the devil.

Jesus never preached the law and the Old Testament prophets but only referred to them, saying, they all wrote about him, and a greater than they had arrived. He acknowledged the laws and prophets, represented by Moses and Elijah, whom he said bye to at the Mount of Transfiguration (Matthew 17:1–13). Jesus said he never came to destroy the law or the prophets but to fulfill them by bringing what the law and the prophets promised—the return of the governing influence of the kingdom of heaven to the earth.

When Jesus sent out his disciples, he did not give room for presumptions but told them exactly what they should preach—the gospel of the kingdom: "And as you go, preach, saying, the Kingdom of heaven is at hand" (Matthew 10:7). It is the same message he paraphrased in the model prayer, "Your kingdom come, Your will be done on earth as it is in heaven" (Matthew 6:10). Even after the resurrection, during his forty-day stay on earth, he preached the same message pertaining to the kingdom of God (Acts 1:3). And when the disciples approached him regarding the signs of his return and the end of the age, Jesus concluded his response, saying, "And this gospel of the kingdom will be preached in all the world as a witness to all nations, and then the end will come" (Matthew 24:14). Based on this, we should not be surprised that the end has not come. We are preaching our own messages contrary to his instructions.

Jesus never missed words when he warned about religious hypocrisy and the deplorable state the scribes and Pharisees were leading the children of Israel, when he said, "But woe to you, scribes and Pharisees, hypocrites! For you shut up the kingdom of heaven against men; for neither go in yourselves, nor do you allow those who are entering to go in" (Matthew 23:13). He also stressed the fact that it is the Father's good pleasure to give us the kingdom to dominate the earth (Luke 12:32). God is pleased to give mankind a government not a religion. Religion does not teach how to rule but how to endure; it does not train people to overcome but makes them comfortable in their depression. That explains why the greatest enemies of Jesus were religious people who substituted the kingdom message for religion and prevented others from entering into it.

Religion came into existence when man fell from dominion. The root word for religion is "to search." So, religion is only necessary if one is lost. Before humans fell, there was no need for religion because they were in the presence of God. Religion is our attempt to find something we believe we lost. To stop our search, God decided to come himself to restore the relationship we had with him and reintroduce us to the governing authority we lost. In the Old Testament, mankind left home and later tried to return through religious works, which emphasized servanthood over sonship. In the new dispensation, Jesus restored us through his death and resurrection as sons and co-workers with the father.

Unfortunately, some believers are like the prodigal son; they return to their father and prefer the position of a servant rather than the glory of a son. The father wants sons, created in his image and likeness, who value their birthright and their inheritance. The calling to sonship in the New Testament is the message of the kingdom that we are expected to preach and teach, not religion!

Religious people disregard the kingdom message because it has a convicting spirit. Religion condemns rather than convicts. It reduces adultery to getting caught. Whereas in the kingdom lust is already a sin, waiting for an opportunity to manifest. The religious leaders who brought the woman caught in adultery were applying religious laws to condemn her to death, but Jesus, who is the fulfillment of the law and Lord of the kingdom of righteousness, brought unto the scene the convicting spirit and all the accusers left without throwing a single stone (John 8:1–11). He then instructed the woman who had been convicted and not condemned to go and sin no more.

God's agenda is to have sons who are citizens of his kingdom—not servants, subjects, or members of religious sects. As sons, we are mandated to represent the government of heaven and its interest on the earth. In this regard, we are obliged to walk in the footsteps of Jesus, teaching and preaching the right gospel of the kingdom to make the earth look like the home country—heaven.

Chapter 20

A New Covenant Assignment—The Shadow and the Substance

Quite often some believers and congregations who launch their new birth experience by faith suddenly find themselves taking a course based on works. They are saved by grace through faith but gradually move into works of the law rather than living exclusively by faith. Under the new covenant, God does not need our works but our belief and trust in the work he has already accomplished for us through Christ Jesus (John 6:29).

Reverting to works of the law cancels grace, which we freely received by faith. In life, once the substance appears the shadow fades away. Paul, in chapter 3 of his epistle to the believers in Galatia, used the principle of the shadow and the substance to describe the purpose of the law of works and grace through faith. From his narrative, we understand that the purpose of the law that was given to Israel through

Moses was to reveal transgressions and their inability to receive the promise made to Abraham by works. The law was not for righteousness but to reveal lawlessness, insubordination and ungodliness (1 Timothy 1:8–9), whereas grace through faith was given as a fulfillment of prophecy of the redemption of mankind through the Seed of Abraham (Genesis 15:5; 22:18; Ephesians 2:8).

Abraham was counted as righteous, not by works of the law, but because he believed God as faithful to keep his promise of a Seed to his descendants who would redeem humankind from the curse of the law (Galatians 3:13–14). Jews and Gentiles who belief in Christ become heirs according to the promise made to Abraham. When God's promise—his Word—became flesh in the form of the man Jesus and dwelled among us, the law, which was the shadow came to an end. That is why the New Testament teaches that Christ is the end of the law (Romans 10:4) and that the law was given through Moses, but grace and truth came through Jesus Christ (John 1:17). "The law was our tutor to bring us to Christ, that we might be justified by faith. But after faith has come, we are no longer under a tutor" (Galatians 3:24–25).

There is a marked difference between the shadow (old covenant) and the substance (new covenant). The law was the shadow, wherein God's people had to do things to appease or impress him, and God in return reciprocated. In the new covenant, however, grace is the substance whereby believers regain their citizenship, understand kingdom principles, and inevitably enjoy the rights and privileges of God's unmerited favor.

The foundation of the old contract was service and reward based, as it is written, "So you shall serve the Lord your God, and He will bless your bread and your water" (Exodus 23:25). By contrast, the new contract is based on grace and inheritance, as narrated by Paul saying, "For by grace you have been saved through faith, and not of yourselves; it is a gift of God, not of works, lest anyone should boast" (Ephesians 2:8). Grace restored us to the wealth the first Adam inherited freely and enjoyed while in Eden, until he disobeyed God and subsequently, the generations that came after him had to serve to be blessed.

There existed a covenant of dominion through obedience between man and God, one that was severed when man declared independence from the home country. When this happened, the seal of our inherited covenant, the Holy Spirit (Ephesians 1:13–14), left the colony and returned to the headquarters in heaven. As a result of the recall of the Holy Spirit and mankind's search for God, the covenant of the law and prophets, referred to as the old covenant, was enacted. This covenant revealed man's sin and helplessness to keep the law without the spirit of the law. It also prepared the ground for the return to the first covenant of obedience that was in the garden of Eden prior to the fall of mankind.

The covenant of the law and prophets was set in the blood of goats and lambs and the people were obliged to gather in a place called the house of God—temples, synagogues, where the Holy Spirit came down to give the people the word of God. God's desire has always been for the Holy Spirit to dwell in man, and not in houses made with bricks, stones, and wood (Acts 7:48). Paul stated this fact when he warned the believers in Corinth against sexual immorality, saying, "Do you not know that your body is the temple of the Holy Spirit who is in you, whom you have received from God, and you are not your own?" (1 Corinthians 6:18–19).

The concept of building houses for God, erecting altars, offering of sacrifices, and even the priesthood establishment, were consequences of the fall. The devil knows that when mankind assumes their rightful position as sons of God, the world will change, and his kingdom's influence will be destroyed. So, he infiltrates the church with pagan practices such as idol worship, giving to receive as opposed to giving out of thanksgiving, sacrificing to earn favor with God as opposed to enjoying his free gift through the death of Jesus.

God has never been pleased by these acts of worship. He always wanted his original stuff—man as the temple of the Holy Spirit walking and talking with him as Daddy and Son. This is what happened in the garden of Eden when God breathed into man his Spirit and eventually at Pentecost when the Holy Spirit descended from heaven and filled the disciples.

The new covenant is the recovery of that which Adam lost in Eden—the indwelling presence of God—the Holy Spirit. Hence, God spoke of restoring the substance we lost, saying, "And it shall come to pass afterward that I will pour out My Spirit on all flesh; your sons and your daughters shall prophesy, your old men shall dream dreams, your young men shall see visions" (Joel 2:28). This was fulfilled first when Jesus breathed the Holy Spirit into the disciples (John 20:22) and secondly with the outpouring of the Holy Spirit at Pentecost (Acts 2:1–4).

We have all it takes to manifest the glory of heaven on earth once again. The second Adam (Jesus) repositioned us into God's presence. We should now turn the great hymns set in old covenant patterns to new covenant renditions. Instead of singing, "God Will Make A Way"[19] let's sing, God has made a way! He did it more than two thousand years ago. Jesus also said, he is the way to the truth that gives us the life of God (John 14:6). We should seek and follow Jesus the way, not keep singing, "Pass Me Not O Gentle Savior"[20] In like manner, we should not continue in the Old Testament pattern of asking God to send his word to heal and deliver us from destructions, but believe that these provisions are done deals on the account of the events at Calvary (Psalm 107:20; John 1:14; 19:30). Our target today is to seek God and his righteousness, avoid the traps of religious practices, and follow the guidance of the Holy Spirit who shows us the things in our lives that are hindering us from overcoming sinful desires, enjoying good health and living in divine provision.

The two contracts (old and new covenants) were separated by a period of more than four hundred years. The statement by Jesus, "It is finished!" at the cross marked the closure of an era and the beginning of another. His resurrection and ascension into heaven returned the Holy Spirit into the law. With the Spirit back in the law, mankind could finally understand God's intention for giving the laws.

The old covenant had run its course. The substance had been restored. By Moses the law was delivered to Israel—Jews, whereas by Jesus grace and truth have been made available to both Jews and gentiles (John 1:17). The laws of Moses revealed the sin nature (rebellion) we had inherited from the fall of Adam, and consequently bore the fruits of lawlessness. But by the grace of Jesus we have re-inherited God's righteous nature and are expected to change and show evidence of transformation by bearing righteous fruits (Galatians 5:16–24).

Lawlessness has inherent punishment while grace also has inherent reward. The law exposes weakness, condemns, and kills whereas grace convicts and redeems us from it. By implication, the result of a mixture or cocktail of the old and new covenant is limited impact.

The covenants can be likened to three cars running on different sources of energy, such as: gas (petrol), renewable energy and a combination of both (cocktail). The car running on gas is effective but not sustainable (Hebrews 8:7), the car running on a combination of gas and renewable energy can easily run into confusion and frustration, as putting new wine in old wineskins (Mark 2:21–22). However, the car running on renewable energy is innovation, it is effective and efficient. Innovation renders old knowledge obsolete, even as it is written, "A new covenant he has made the first obsolete" (Hebrews 8:13).

Believers who want to be effective in this new era or dispensation should seek to understand the terms of the new covenant gospel of the kingdom and only refer to the old for reference purposes. We should do away with old practices that have no place in the new dispensation and look only unto Jesus with the help and guidance of the Holy Spirit. Doing the reverse, is living in the shadow or cocktail, whereas the substance is here. We should follow the footsteps of Jesus who in his days commanded his followers to preach, teach the gospel of the kingdom and restore the heavenly kingdom government back to earth not by works or religious practices but by grace. We are in the last days, therefore, the true and uncorrupted gospel of the kingdom must be preached.

The Jews were called out and led by the law and the prophets to be an example to Gentile nations. During that time, the Spirit of God came upon the prophets and qualified them to speak on behalf of God and lead the people. But under the new dispensation of grace, Jesus said, "But the hour is coming, and now is, when the true worshipers will worship the Father in spirit and truth: for the Father is seeking such to worship Him. God is Spirit and those who worship Him must worship in spirit and truth" (John 4:23– 24).

All believers have the Spirit of God dwelling in them, to teach, counsel and guide them. In that regard, the assignment of the ministers in the fivefold ministry is to equip the believers to listen to the indwelling Counselor and follow his guidance and manifest the kingdom as they go about their responsibilities (Ephesians 4:11–12).

God established the assembly of believers (church) as a cabinet that would foster the return of his government that was lost to the prince of darkness. Regrettably, this assignment has been derailed by pagan practices and branded as a religion, to say but the least. The king of glory has been misrepresented as a religious figure and his political agenda turned into religious organizations.

As ambassadors of the kingdom, we should shine as lights and cities on hills that cannot be hidden. We need to believe in the finished work of Jesus and understand our new covenant assignment to avoid mixture because we have the Spirit of God dwelling in us to empower us to impact the earth with the culture of heaven (John 14:12).

Chapter 21

Political and Church Leadership

Jesus is not a religious leader, nor did he command his followers to construct buildings called houses of God. The "house of God" was an Old Testament concept where the people of Israel gathered to worship and received God's council via chosen prophets or priests. The counselor, governor from heaven, the Holy Spirit, at that point in time could not dwell in man, so he came down occasionally and inspired God's messengers to convey his message to his people.

After the ascension of Jesus, the governor descended from heaven and established himself in the assembly of believers at Pentecost and as a result, the church was born. On the account of these events, the assembly of believers in whom the Holy Spirit dwells became the church—the body of Christ (1 Corinthians 3:16). This assembly is what Jesus commissioned before ascending into heaven and reminded them that they were and still are the light of the world. Their light, which is the knowledge of the truth, is expected to shine before men, that they may see their good works—not wealth, buildings, relics or words—and glorify the father in heaven (Matthew 5:13–16).

This commissioned assembly is yet to fully mature and manifest its glory. The late Dr. Myles Munroe vividly described church immaturity this way, "The church is approximately 2,000 years old and yet not matured; it has excitement without depth; great anointing without character; power without principles; gifts without standards; fleshy without faith; meetings without first meeting with God; God is demanding maturity and responsibility."[21] Things should and must change!

For the church to manifest its glory, it needs to acknowledge the presence of the Holy Spirit, the source and author of power. Jesus knew every person on earth is seeking power to control circumstances, especially the storms of life, both natural and spiritual. Man lost the power to subdue or govern the earth and all therein. Jesus understood this and promised a power release upon the disciples before they could embark on their mission to conquer the world. He commanded them to wait in Jerusalem for the promise of the father and in so doing, they would receive power when the Holy Spirit came upon them and they would be witnesses to him in Jerusalem, and in all Judea and Samaria, and to the end of the earth (Acts 1:4, 8).

Power, like knowledge without the truth, can be acquired cheaply. But real power which is authorized from above can only be given by the Holy Spirit. Satan and his demons have unauthorized power and corrupted wisdom which they use to lure and destroy many.

World leaders, politicians and many religious figures are desperate for power to make a difference in their lives, communities, and nations. Many join cults and practice all manner of satanic and demonic rituals just to get power. One needs to see the chaotic scramble for whatever power there is during election period in many countries. Some leaders opt for fake versions of power because many at times the real "power brokers"—the church—cannot offer them the true version that Jesus promised and restored through the return of the Holy Spirit.

Another dilemma is the separation of church business and politics. It is like an "organized mafia." Politicians know when and how to use the church for their own gain. Constantine the first Christian emperor of Rome, capitalized on the derogatory name (Christians) given by pagans to the early church to gain political mileage and achieve greatness. His maneuver made the 'church' and Christianity the religion of Rome. His first strategy was to proclaim that he had converted to Christianity and then moved to merge the church and state. This was a diabolic move because the church is an assembly of believers not Christians and therefore not a religion. The church constitutes of a political assembly of ambassadors representing the government of heaven on earth. Hence, the church is above the state, and state government should take its cue from church government.

When Constantine succeeded in his political gamble, the people of Rome brought with them their pagan practices into the church and repackaged their idol gods with Christian names. The Roman gods Jupiter, Isis, Hermes were renamed Peter, Mary, and Christ the good shepherd, respectively. Instead of the church converting the heathen world, pagans converted the church and the church was plunged into apostasy[22]. The church began to drink the cup of the Lord and the cup of demons (1 Corinthians 10:21).

The church is yet to fully recover from the treachery of Constantine the great. It is resistant to change and remains at the "Mount of Transfiguration," reliving traditions and building structures, while down in the valley unbelieving politicians continue to make laws that go against the known will of God, thereby wreaking havoc among the captives, akin to the transfiguration story in Matthew 17.

Religious folks and some believers may be quick to say things like, politics is a dirty game but would not dare to change the players and provide an alternative to clean up the mess. As ambassadors of the kingdom of Heaven, this is no longer an option for us, we must bring that heavenly change and proclaim the victory we have through Christ Jesus. Politics is neutral, it is the "players" that are dirty not the "game." In the words of George Orwell, "a people that elect corrupt politicians, imposters, thieves and traitors are not victims but accomplices."[23]

A wise judge described politics in quite simple terms. He said, "Politics is the process by which a society chooses the rules that will govern it. Through politics we choose our political system (kingdom, democracy, socialism etc.); we choose our constitution and finally our political leaders."[24] Politics therefore is the pulse of life. Our lives, families, communities, and nations need policies that bring order and prosperity. This can only be achieved through the alignment of our policies to kingdom principles by participatory process of all and sundry.

There have been several outcries by Christians across the globe, against world leaders who are supposedly standing up against religion and calling for the closure of churches in their nations. Some leaders have gone as far as openly telling religious leaders, church goers and "men of God" to stay away from politics. Why is it so, if the drive is the same—good policies, good governance, and prosperity for all citizens? The church needs to have a soul search. Could it be that the God they claim to know and serve is using these leaders to tell them to wake up and focus on the correct assignment and refrain from witch-hunting world leaders for standing against religion, the very thing that God warned against?

Think about it. May be things could be different, if the church was giving these leaders what they are looking for—the ability to overcome circumstances, personal security and fulfillment, kingdom citizenship and authorized power. Then probably they would be rushing into the kingdom just as Nicodemus did when he heard Jesus talking about kingdom citizenship and power. This Jewish leader came to Jesus looking for the kingdom power Jesus preached about, not heaven, "fire insurance" or "bless me Lord." Many leaders are like Nicodemus;

they are looking for power to rule, not religion to appease a god. They are not even looking for Jesus but what he brought—authorized power. When the church fails to deliver the power these leaders are craving for, they then head to unauthorized dealers and receive unauthorized power which eventually destroys them and the people, the church inclusive.

Let us not forget that church growth accelerates under pressure and persecution. These forces can be used to fuel and propel the church to take up positions of authority and bring the kingdom's culture to them. As the eagle uses thermals to soar higher, so should the church use opposition to advance the cause of the kingdom. A Pharisee, named Gamaliel, advised those who sought to persecute the church by saying, "For if this plan or this work is of men, it will come to nothing: but if it is of God, you cannot overthrow it—lest you even be found to fight against God" (Acts 5:38–39). This is in line with what Jesus said concerning his church: "I will build My church, and the gates of Hades shall not prevail against it" (Matthew 16:18).

Several world leaders and politicians do not know where they are leading the world to. A utopia or dystopia? They need knowledge, wisdom, and direction from a prevailing church not from religious organizations. The church needs to believe in the message they are propagating, before presenting it to the world. With that, they should self-assess by listening to the Spirit of Truth in order to offer valid contributions that address world issues. The church and the state need to also understand that the future of the world is behind us and not in front. They need to acknowledge God's popular and paradoxical prefix re-: "Return to me and I will return to you, says the Lord of hosts" (Malachi 3:7). The utopia that humanity is desperately looking for can only be found in the Eden model of leadership which is self-government with God's laws written in our hearts and the Lord as our king, judge and law giver (Isaiah 33:22).

Democratic nations and republics have adopted the three arms of government—executive, judiciary and legislative—but have developed humanistic constitutions rather than constitutions based on God's moral code and law, and the Lord who sits in heaven laughs (Psalm 2:1–5). Leadership by majority may be good but not necessarily right. Many at times the majority vote is wrong, and politicians become victims of crowds and popular opinions, and the cost is often grievous, akin to the popular demand made by Israel for an earthly king (1 Samuel 8).

Bad government is the product of moral erosion and development without divine direction and above all, the absence of the fear of God. These traits lead to disorder, discontentment, rebellion, and chaos. Spending billions trying to fix bad government never works. We need a different approach to governance, as that which Adam lost, and Jesus restored. The focus of Jesus was kingdom governing authority, it was irreligious and focused on all the systems of the state which served the people rather than extracting from them.

When the kingdom is preached to the captives, poor and sick, they arise and take charge of their lives and the dependency syndrome is solved. This is why God is more concerned with mental revolution rather than religious rituals. Religion makes people comfortable in their misery and dependent. Whereas the kingdom message transforms people's minds to contribute to society. The earth and the systems upon it await those with authorized power to set things in order (Romans 8:19).

The church has the eminent responsibility of liberating the world from oppression through the application of the transforming message of the return of the kingdom of heaven. It has the mandate to bring knowledge of the truth to individuals, families, communities, and nations that are still in bondage because they are ignorant of these key truths:

> ➤ We were delivered from the bondage of sin, more than two thousand years ago by a deliverer—Jesus
> ➤ We were redeemed by the blood of Jesus, healed by his stripes, and blessed by his rejection.
> ➤ Our enemy, the devil, like a toothless bulldog is under our feet.

Because of the ignorance of the finished work of Jesus at the cross, many continue to ask God to send a deliverer, his word, and blessings, and these have consequently led to performance-based acts. In other words, doing things to convince, beg and manipulate God. Ignorance of these truths thrusts us to retain the Old Testament model of fighting the battles of life. This old dispensation method of fighting involved men of war in the battlefield fighting flesh and blood.

In the new dispensation, we fight the good fight of faith, where our victory is a done deal as God is the one who fights our battles and disarms our enemies (1 Timothy 6:12; John 16:33). Men, women, and children in this new dispensation war in the spirit realms with the Word of God, praying against principalities and evoking the angels of God to destroy satanic forces operating in other humans. Therefore, instead of cursing and condemning other humans, the church and state should work together to call for national prayers to subdue and expel unauthorized powers operating in the land.

The church and state are expected to work hand in glove for the prosperity of all citizens. Both should be involved and fully participate in all national processes to choose a system of government, formulate government policies and laws, elect political leaders, and implement all government key functions that include:

> Maintaining order in societies, by establishing godly policies and laws to help citizens discover and accomplish their purposes, thereby guaranteeing individual success and national development.
> Establishing effective educational systems at all levels where citizens identify and refine their purpose for existence and acquire the necessary skills for personal and national development.

> ➤ Fostering true leadership development by creating a robust and thriving environment for everyone to discover self and the right to function in that capacity.

Leadership at all levels of society are established by God to partner with him to train, guide and influence individuals, families, communities, and nations to fulfil his purpose for their existence. Righteous leaders exercise the authority given to them by God to maintain law and order. When such leaders are in power, the people rejoice. They are guided by God's vision, which transcends generations. They do not invent a vision but simply align to it and commit to developing other leaders to carry the vision forward.

On the other hand, unrighteous leaders are not in right standing with God, they have their personal ambitions, thrive in ignorance, breed division, and maintain followers with the grip of fear and oppression. Developing future leaders is never on their agenda, which is why when they rule, the people groan and cast-off restraint (Proverbs 29:2, 18). Therefore, let the sons of God arise and take on the dominion assignment of making the earth and its systems function like heaven.

Chapter 22

Kingdom Authority

The concept of kingdom authority needs clarification given that the Bible is a kingdom book inspired by the Holy Spirit whose message is mainly about a kingdom and its culture. This kingdom message confers or delegates authority to mankind to dominate the earth. In that regard, kingdom authority is the right or permission entrusted to mankind to make and enforce decisions in the colony on behalf of the king.

The absence and misconception of kingdom culture today makes the message of Jesus exceedingly difficult to understand. Most Europeans, Asians and Africans have had experiences with kingdoms and can relate to an extent with the kingdom message and the concept of kingdom colonization. However, they too find it difficult to receive, comprehend and apply the kingdom of God's culture here on the earth. Kingdoms unlike other forms of government differ greatly in structure and functions. Some of the distinctive features of kingdoms include the following:

- ➤ The king is the ultimate authority in a kingdom.
- ➤ The king is born king, unlike presidents, prime ministers, and political leaders, who are voted into authority.
- ➤ The king's word is law, and his laws are his mind on paper.
- ➤ The king owns everything, including the people in the kingdom, as personal property.
- ➤ The king chooses the citizens and becomes totally responsible for them. But in a democracy, the people choose the president and work for everything.
- ➤ The king is totally responsible for the citizens' welfare because their success is tied to his reputation. Therefore, worrying in a kingdom is saying that the king is irresponsible.
- ➤ As owner of everything in the kingdom, the king can favor and give anything to any citizen freely. However, a president cannot because it will be considered as corruption.
- ➤ In a kingdom, subjects must show absolute obedience and loyalty to the throne, whereas democracy requires cooperation with authority.

Kingdoms give citizenship and citizenship give rights, privileges, and authority. Once citizenship is conferred upon individuals, they are given the keys or secrets of the kingdom's culture and they demonstrate their love for the king and his kingdom by keeping the laws of the country.

Kingdoms have three significant symbols: crowns, sensors, and scepters. They represent power, influence, and authority, respectively. The most important is the scepter because it is the symbol of authority in a kingdom (Genesis 49:10; Esther 4:11; Psalm 45:6). Authority is conferred upon an individual by another in a higher position.

Many people are mesmerized and swayed by power, but one must examine if it is authorized or not. Some so called men of God have power without authority; that's why Jesus said that they call him "Lord, Lord" but he never sent them. Power can then be defined as the ability to do something. Authority, on the other hand, is the right or permission to carry out the assignment.

A person with authorized power is more effective than one with power alone. The devil is not afraid of your power but your authority, so do not pursue power but authority. The authority by which God sent Moses, gave his rod the power to swallow the power in the rods of Pharaoh's magicians. Jesus received authority from God and conferred upon the believer the same authority his Father had conferred upon him (Luke 22:29; Matthew 28:18–19). It is also by divine authority that Jesus could take back the authority over the kingdoms that were lost by man, from the devil.

The devil had authority over the kingdoms of the earth because Adam disobeyed, and as a result, handed over the authority or dominion entrusted to him by God in the beginning to the devil. This is substantiated by what satan told Jesus: "All this authority I will give You, and their glory: for this has been delivered to me, and I give it to whomever I wish" (Luke 4:6).

Kingdom authority makes the power in the written word effective. When you believe in Jesus and submit to the written word, God gives you the power of attorney to use the name of Jesus to subdue the enemy (Philippians 2:9–10). Any use of the name of Jesus without submitting to God's Word and authority yields no effect.

In the world, humans have authority and God has the power. In the beginning God gave man authority when he said, "Let them have dominion…" God has all the power to do anything on earth, but he needs us to authorize him. A man of God once said, "Without God man cannot, and without man, God will not."[25]

God manifested his authority and power through Jesus and that provoked the chief priests, scribes and elders to confront him, saying, "Tell us, by what authority are You doing these things? Or who is he who gave You this authority?" (Luke 20:2). They never questioned his power but his authority. They were comfortable ascribing his power to that of the ruler of demons than to that of God (Matthew 12:24).

Demons do not fear power but authority. If you have power without authority demons will say to you, as they said to the seven sons of Sceva, "Jesus I know, and Paul I know; but who are you?" (Acts 19:14–15). One in authority does not need to be in your presence for things to be done. All they have to do is command from any location what is expected to happen, because they have the backing of the headquarters. That is why Jesus marveled at the centurion's comprehension of the relationship between authority and power. The Centurion understood that authority makes power authentic and that Jesus had authority from heaven even as he had authority vested upon him by the Roman government to execute duties in its colony (Matthew 8:5–13).

Everyone is born with a personal gift to exercise authority over their sphere of life, otherwise called territorial dominion. So, we should always ask God to reveal to us our area of influence to obtain true success. In that area, God will not forsake nor leave us (Joshua 1:5). Therefore, we are not to compare or imitate others who are in their own spheres. We are to learn from them while retaining our unique personality. The world has enough counterfeit products, so we are not to add to them, because the enemy will challenge us once we step into other people's territories.

God gives you his character first and second a dominion assignment and then demands stewardship. You need dominion power to become a good steward because the enemy is always contesting your stewardship mandate. This mandate requires the finding of new ways to do old things or considering new methods to solve old problems, never wasting resources but combining them to create new things for the glory of the kingdom.

When God gives you authority then you are authorized to be authentic. A bird is an authentic flyer. It has authority to fly from the Creator. In the area of gifting, one must pursue and submit to divine authority to function effectively. Pursuit of unauthorized power is rebellious in nature and treasonous in the kingdom. Anything you try to do without authority will easily destroy you. This is evident in various vices, such as imitation, which rob you of your authentic self or your unique contribution to society.

In like manner, anyone exercising kingdom authority on behalf of the King needs to be authentic not just anointed. Being anointed does not necessarily mean you are authorized. David said King Saul was the anointed one, even though God had disowned him as king of Israel. God had left Saul even as he leaves some anointed preachers who are living in sin and still performing miracles. Therefore, be careful to be under the right authority and not just under anointing. For God's gifts and his calling are irrevocable (Romans 11:29).

The world disciplines and even jails people who do not respect authority but some people in the church abuse authority all week, then sit under disqualified pastors saying amen. It is foolishness to submit to people who are themselves not submitted to authority. That is why we have the Holy Spirit who constantly sounds alarms when we are making questionable choices and submitting to unauthorized power.

Authority and power dynamics apply in marriages and families. These principles revolve around the ingredients of delegated power, love, and submission. In the family, the male man, as father, is designed to show the children how the heavenly father is. As a husband, he shows the wife how Jesus is, and she then shows the husband how the church should be (Ephesians 5:22–33).

Marriage and family are divine setups and should obey divine principles. They need attention because they are the foundation of the society. As the very fabric of life, marriage and the family constitute the foundation of the society and impact the culture of the nation.

The husband has delegated authority and hence the head of the family. The wife, like the neck, helps to turn the head. She is highly favored to influence and incubate the vision and plans of the family. She is the man's helper, not a partner. The children are like hair that eventually leave the head, one way or another. The family vision from God that the man carries should be supported by the rest of the family, and in so doing they also obtain fulfillment in their lives.

Your strength is where God positions you. No man should craft an ambition and then try to coax or manipulate the rest of the family to submit to it. Sarah called Abraham, her husband, lord, or master because Abraham was submitted to God and that relationship influenced how he took care of her. The head of the family is responsible for the family because every male is responsible 100 percent for whatever carries his name. In a marriage the wife does not leave her father and mother, but simply shifts from one father to another. That is why she takes on the name of the husband. "Headship" is not tyranny but responsibility; and "helper-ship" is not partner-ship but influence.

In the Old Testament or covenant, one could simply take a divorce by the courts who issued a certificate to annul the union. The Pharisees said to Jesus, "Moses permitted a man to write a certificate of divorce, and to dismiss her." Jesus answered and said to them, "Because of the hardness of your heart he wrote you this precept. But from the beginning of the creation, God made them male and female" (Mark 10:4–6). This was the New Testament precept Jesus brought into marriage. He reintroduced the spirit of the law back into the institution of marriage by stating the original intention.

In the old dispensation, the marriage institution was based on the law of Moses and the prophets. A marriage certificate was issued under the law to protect the parties involved. This notion of marriage certificate showed just how far man had fallen from the kingdom's values and morals. There is no account of God issuing a marriage certificate to Adam and Eve. He simply witnessed the coming together of two whole individuals and completed the "triangle of marriage."

However, when man fell from dominion, the everlasting covenant of marriage that involved God, the male and female was severed and had to be restored by Jesus. Contrary, to what most of the Jews at the time expected, Jesus announced that he did not come to do away with the law but to fulfill all that was spoken about him by all the prophets. This meant that, in the new dispensation, Christ became the end of the law. That is, he fulfilled all works of the law so that we could access all that God had already destined for us by grace (Romans 10:4; Matthew 5:17).

To that end, we are no longer under the law but grace and truth that came through Jesus (John 1:17). So, when it comes to relationships, we are to love one another in the New

Testament way, as God loves us. Marriages and the in-law support system should take on the New Testament model. The two become one flesh, in an everlasting covenant by grace and the in-law support system becomes an "in-Christ" or "in-grace" support system, wherein the father, mother, brothers, sisters, etc. become the "in-Christ" as opposed to in-laws. They support the marriage institution by understanding and applying the grace of Jesus not by the law of Moses, which condemns, but by grace, which convicts and forgives.

Marriage is fueled by love and candor (truth), not by diplomacy and external interference. The two become one flesh, and no one is permitted to put asunder what God has put together (Mark 10:8–9). Hence if you want to marry, do it God's way or stay alone, as Paul said and did (1 Corinthians 7:8). Being a husband and wife—head and helper, position, and influencer—are duties assigned by God. These were inherently endowed by the Creator to our first parents as complementary differences for them to better serve their gifts. Marriage is then not a partnership. The principles of marriage existed before we arrived and will be there when we leave. All principles and laws have inherent consequences and rewards. If we desire a new formula to marriage, we should avoid plagiarism and craft a name for it, establish the principles and accept the consequences.

The male was formed to lead by virtue of position, while the female by influence. Influence is more powerful than position. Influence rules without sitting on the throne, what some have termed "pillow politics" akin to the story of Jezebel and king Ahab (1 Kings 21:5–8). The devil understands this power of influence in the female and usually goes after her to desta-bilize the man in position. To destroy a community, the enemy usually seeks to destroy the strong man—the male. The male position is vulnerable and often targeted for destruction.

In the United States, for example, the father's rights are at the bottom in the home, while the child's is first and mother is between. Protecting the child and mother's rights is good, but two wrongs never make a right. On the flip side, in Africa and other parts of the world, the principle of the male position as head of the family is often misconstrued and has morphed into male dominance and tyranny.

Let us learn to obey divine principles and keep our fami-lies and communities safe. The survival and wellbeing of our nations are tied to how we understand and apply kingdom authority and power. We have the sole objective to pursue the king and his interest for the colony, with the ultimate purpose of making the colony function like heaven.

Chapter 23

Kingdom Laws of Power

Our understanding of kingdom authority is key to comprehend and apply the concept of kingdom laws of power.
In the context of this chapter, laws can simply be defined as
the sets of rules that govern the operations and functioning
of individuals, communities, and states. Power on the other
hand is the ability, energy, force, and enablement or anointing to do something. The source of all laws that authorize and
govern the ability to get things done is more important than
power.

Source and Purpose of Power

Whether we know, ignore, believe, doubt, agree or disagree,
the reality is that the laws which govern human power take
root from two sources—the kingdom of light and that of darkness. The kingdom of light is a domain where knowledge of

the truth of oneself, the Creator and all his creation prevails. Whereas the kingdom of darkness is the domain of ignorance, deception, seduction, and manipulation. These two kingdoms or jurisdictions are ruled by two different authorities. You and I are influenced by either.

Jesus Christ is the king and light of the domain of truth. He declared, "I am the light of the world; He who follows Me shall not walk in darkness, but have the light of life" (John 8:12). Satan, the devil is the ruler of the kingdom of darkness. He is also called the great dragon, the god of this age, the prince of the power of the air, the compulsive spirit that works in the sons of disobedience (Revelation 12:9; Ephesians 2:2).

Prior to the fall of our first parents in the garden of Eden, they had dominion power over the earth and all therein, given to them by the Creator. Before they received power, God gave them his nature and character. Hence Adam and Eve were to execute power in line with the nature and laws of God. For that to happen, they needed to maintain their relationship with the father. This also can be referred to as righteousness or right standing with the Creator, which they lost when they disobeyed his word, an act masterminded by satan.

In the previous chapters we narrated how Lucifer lost his place in heaven through a rebellion and failed coup d'état against divine authority, and was kicked out of heaven. As he fell, he took up residence in the colony—the earth. Despite these events, the devil still craved for power and influence. He hatched a rebellion and out maneuvered Adam and Eve, by introducing them to power that was apart from God and a desire to be like God, knowing good and evil (Genesis 3:5). This resulted in their fall from dominion and his rise to power.

In the beginning God never wanted mankind to know good and evil but good. Considering that, when one knows good and evil without passing the obedience test and submitting oneself to divine authority, evil tends to prevail. The test of obedience is the platform of the knowledge and the choice between good and evil. When Adam and Eve failed the obedience test, evil prevailed and set the course for self-aggrandizement and humanism.

Satan's maneuver and trickery did not catch God unaware. This only set the pace for the implementation of God's alternate plan to salvage and restore humankind to their original position of divine power. As a starting point, God called several men to walk with him and finally chose a prototype nation and gave them laws to awaken their conscience to the nature and consequences of evil, because where there is no law there cannot be sin and imputation.

The laws of Moses and the prophets were intended to reveal sin, not to solve the sin problem. External laws only awaken one's conscience to sin and expose the helplessness to keep such laws. The solution to the sin problem required a power working from within to transform the conscience (Romans 12:2). This power is the spirit of the law.

In the field of law, the spirit of the law is the intention, purpose, and backbone of the law. The law of God also has a spirit, called the Holy Spirit. God's law and his Spirit constitute the law of righteousness that leads to eternal life. The law of God without the Spirit is called the law of sin and death (Romans 8:1–3). Without this Spirit, no one can successfully keep the law of God. This explains why, Jesus had to pay the price of Adam and Eve's disobedience, which had left humans void of the Holy Spirit—the governor within, who enables one to live from the inside out (self- or internal governance) rather than from the outside in. The sacrifice of Jesus, our belief in him and the return of the Holy Spirit into mankind are fundamental to self-governance and the fulfillment of the dominion mandate.

Laws without the Holy Spirit require policing and fear of reprisals to maintain them. The so-called constitutional laws that are expected to govern, control, and regulate human lives are in reality rules and traditions of men. They are difficult to develop, implement, maintain or even defend because the spirit of the author is not within such laws, to empower citizens to adhere to them. These "laws" do not speak to the heart (the subconscious mind) but rather to the flesh—emotions and feelings, which depend on external inputs and senses. Consequently, they wane like new-year resolutions and behavior change seminars.

If humanity desires real change it must embrace the divine agent of change, the Holy Spirit, who transforms us from the inside out. He reveals to us the very nature of God and endows us with the ability to use power as originally intended. Power that is void of divine principles and laws is the premise for deception and manipulation of other humans.

Temptations of Power

"It seems easier to be God than to love God, easier to control people than to love people, easier to own life than to love life".[26] Hardly would you hear anyone say, "I was tempted to do good," rather, "I was overwhelmed by the temptation to do wrong." This is because we lost the very essence of love, the nature of God which gives us the power to love ourselves and others.

God is love, and power without love is tyranny. The craving of power caused Lucifer to lose his place in heaven. He became the prince of darkness, the master of deception, seduction, manipulation, and control. He is also the compulsive spirit that works in the sons of disobedience, causing them to lust after power to control others and events.

Deception is the most potent weapon of diabolic power. It derives all its actions from the evil one and gradually corrupts and destroys the character of the bearer. Abraham Lincoln said, "Nearly all men can stand adversity, but if you want to test a man's character, give him power."[27] God invariably gave humans his nature and character before giving them power to dominate circumstances and not other people. Without God's character, misuse of power is inevitable.

History has a myriad of "gods of power" from ancient Greek to Egypt. Their worshippers revered them out of fear of reproach as opposed to love. However, God is the source of all power but chooses love over compulsion. That is why the currency of the kingdom of God is not power but love. Power is cheap, love is insurmountable and sacrificial. The thirst for power is insatiable. No one is ever tempted to love people but to control them, think about it. Mahatma Gandhi had this to say, "The day the power of love overrules the love of power, the world will know peace."[28] No wonder Jesus—the epitome of love for mankind, is called the Prince of Peace, peace that surpasses all understanding (Isaiah 9:6; Philippians 4:7). However, this Prince does not impose his reign.

God tests, satan tempts. God tests for weaknesses to promote, while the devil tempts to steal, kill, and destroy (John 10:10). God tested Abraham to sacrifice his son to demonstrate love and obedience and it was accounted to him as righteousness (Genesis 15:6). Whereas satan tempted Adam and Eve, Peter, and Judas Iscariot to do evil, with the sole intention of destroying their destinies (Genesis 3; Luke 22).

Power in the kingdom of God is regulated by his Word, which he has exalted above himself. The same power has been bestowed unto the sons of righteousness. However, where an original exists there is a counterfeit. No one in recent memory has documented the art of deception, seduction, and manipulation to gain power and influence like Robert Greene. His writings reveal the compulsive spirit of Machiavelli and Jezebel that continue to lurk in all realms of power.

Countless books on the genre of power and manipulation have been authored, and the grounds for applying such diabolic laws have never been so present throughout the world systems as seen in today's society. Books such as "The 48 Laws of Power" by Robert Greene[29], offer or guide anyone who wants unauthorized power, observes or wants to arm themselves against the manipulations of power. Greene's book has been referred to by numerous media outlets and admirers as the "Hollywood backstabber's Bible" and described by personalities such as Dov Charney as the "Bible for atheists", he also says of Greene, "I call him Jesus."[30] Statements such as these display just how far the devil is willing to go to compel man against their God-given assignment. These laws spell out over three thousand years of the history of power, zooming in on the lives of those who instead of using power for good, stole, manipulated, killed, and destroyed to protect their reputations. A practice completely different from the example Jesus set and encouraged many to imitate; when he said, "Love your enemies, do good to those who hate you, bless those who curse you, and pray for those who spitefully use you" (Luke 6:27-28).

Power when used according to the prescription of the Creator is like a controlled flame. However, many view it simply as a political tool, which is not the case. Power, like a flame, has many sparks and when abused morphs into an uncontrollable beast. The type of power and seduction depicted in these books are not something new (Ecclesiastes 1:9). They are reminiscence of Jezebel and her evil spirit in biblical history. The Bible holds accounts of this in the first and second book of Kings—a political arena and a befitting place to either use power for good or evil. Jezebel was the daughter of Ethbaal a priest of Baal and king of Tyre/Sidon, modern day Lebanon. She was betrothed and married to Ahab, king of Israel. A marriage built on alliance for protection of the kingdoms. Jezebel's idol worshiping background influenced and caused Ahab to sin against God by leading the prototype nation of Israel into Baal worship (1 Kings 16:31), and their reign over Israel has been described as one of the saddest chapters in the history of God's people.

Jezebel was so evil that the traits of her infamous and obsessive passion for dominion and control of others, especially in the spirit realm, was and is still referred to as the spirit of Jezebel. Her single-minded determination to have her way, no matter who was destroyed in the process is what this manipulative spirit exudes (1Kings 21). Perhaps, the best way to identify the Jezebel spirit is to observe the following characteristics of anyone acting in the same manner as Jezebel, which are; engaging in immorality, idolatry, false teaching, and unrepentant sin. Unfortunately, the end for those who succumb to a Jezebel spirit is always death and destruction, both in the physical and the spiritual sense.

One may wonder, how is this spirit alive and well in this century being that she lives no more? The devil is an impersonator. So, whatever God does, he will duplicate no matter the cost. God sent John the Baptist in the spirit of Elijah (Luke 1:17) because spirits do not die, they simply return to their source. So did the devil, who knows he cannot force us to do the wrong thing but uses the Jezebel spirit to compel, lure and destroy.

Spirits, unlike the bodies that host them, never die. Same applies to the spirit of Jezebel. It is alive and well today and working through humans be they in the church, religious or political systems. Greene or any other person could have fallen victim. We should therefore, be mindful not to quickly casti-gate others for submitting to the spirit of Jezebel. This decep-tive spirit dominated the politics of Israel in the Old Testament and was so infamous in the New Testament church that the Lord Jesus refers to Jezebel in a warning to the church at Thy-atira (Revelation 2:18–29). Despite this warning, the spirit of Jezebel continues to extend its conniving tentacles in the world today.

Many leaders are drunk with the "wine" of Jezebel's spirit. They are wreaking havoc and going against the written laws of God. Various spiritual leaders are mesmerizing and seducing followers with miracles, pretending to be removing the speck in the followers' eyes whilst ignoring the plank in their own eyes (Luke 6:42). They fly the banner of deliverance, instant healings, rain of money and prosperity without consistency, diligence, or work, and gradually slip hooks into the jaws of the ignorant, poor, and greedy. Like fish they are drawn out unto sandy shores where they lie helpless, gasping for air.

The temptation for power is so great that many are lured and will go to any length to acquire it. Once in the corridors of power, many refuse to relinquish it because they have latched on to the source of power, which influences change and commands things to be. However, Power is a neutral force like most of the resources provided to us by God. Just because one has the power to change things does not mean there are no consequences allotted to their decisions. For instance, wa-ter and heat work together to provide precipitation which in return sustains life. One may have the power to drain the water sources and cut down the trees, however, the disruption of these cycles have inherent consequences which do not vanish. All resources in the world, including power are governed by laws, all of which when taken out of balance produce inbuilt consequences. In that regard, power that ignores divine laws and authority is self-destructive in nature. One who disregards the divine laws of power gains mileage and rises to the top only in preparation for a great fall, like satan who fell like lightening from heaven (Luke 10:18).

It is not my intention to analyze and criticize codified laws that are based on writings dating back thousands of years and the experiences of people who excelled or failed at wielding power with glorious or bloody results, but to simply make known the rule of law being applied knowingly or unknowingly to the people in the world today. Diabolic power is a game and rewards are attained according to hierarchy regardless of where it is applied. In The 48 Laws of Power, the author contends that since you cannot opt out of the game of power, you are better off becoming a master player by learning the rules and strategies practiced since ancient times. The literature insinuates that people cannot stand to be powerless. Everyone wants power, be it in the family, government or even the church. The issue at stake is not simply that of power in itself but its origin, laws, and purpose.

The desire for power is natural, because that is what man lost and Jesus promised and restored—dominion over circumstances and not other humans. If power was not of any relevance, then God would not have promised it, neither would he have given it to us (Luke 24:49; Acts 1:8). The source and laws of power are crucial. Jesus never missed his words when he declared the ultimate source of power—the Holy Spirit. He said, "But you shall receive power when the Holy Spirit has come upon you" (Acts 1:8). The Holy Spirit is the presence and revealer of the secrets of God's law and power. He is the only licensed adviser and regulator of the power that dwell within us.

We need to use the lens of the Spirit of God to read and understand the diabolic laws of power documented in the many books on power and influence. Books such as Greene's, imply self-rule and superiority of one's self over all, including God.

Excellency of Power

The laws that govern power are good but the inappropriate use of them is the concern. Abuse is always the case when the mind of the author of laws that regulate power is not known, recognized, or ignored. The Creator is the source of all laws of power. He sets the fundamental principles to execute power and underlines the inherent consequences of abuse.

Contrary to how laws of power have been postulated and documented, Jesus expressed a different view. He demonstrated and advocated for love, compassion, integrity, humility, and servant leadership. He earnestly requested and even instructed his followers to do more than he did because he had connected them to the source of all righteous laws of power.

He said, "Most assuredly, I say to you he who believes in Me, the works that I do he will do also; and greater works than these he will do, because I go to My Father" (John 14:12). He knew how to mentor followers, delegate power and pass on the baton. At a point in his earthly life, Jesus despite the authority and power he possessed called his followers friends and said he would lay down his life for their sake, and expected them to love one another just as he had loved them (John 15:13–16).

Jesus, speaking after his resurrection, reiterated that all authority (delegated power) in heaven and earth had been given to him (Matthew 28:18), and he bestowed upon us the kingdom governing authority, just as the father bestowed one upon him (Luke 22:29). When his disciples asked him saying, "Who then is the greatest in the kingdom of heaven?" Jesus called a little child to Him, set him in the midst of them, and said, "Assuredly, I say to you, unless you are converted and become like little children, you will by no means enter the kingdom of heaven. Therefore whoever humbles himself as this little child is the greatest in the kingdom of heaven" (Matthew 18:1–4). He then followed up and demonstrated servant leadership when he washed his disciples' feet. Upon completion he said to them, "Do you know what I have done to you? You call me Teacher and Lord ..., if then your Lord and Teacher, have washed your feet, you ought to wash one another's feet. For I have given you an example that you should do as I have done to you" (John 13:12–15).

The excellency of power is depicted by Christ's decision to set aside his heavenly glory, humble himself and take on the form of a man to die for the sins of mankind. Obedience to God, love for one another and humility to serve others are keys to exaltation (Philippians 2:5–11). Power is then a byproduct of the restored kingdom of God on the earth and not an instrument of compulsion, manipulation, and self-aggrandizement. Jesus speaking to the guests in the house of a Pharisee said, "For whoever exalts himself will be humbled, and he who humbles himself will be exalted" (Luke 14:11). Diabolic laws of power put into reverse the teaching of the Lord Jesus because they focus on self-exaltation, deception, and manipulation. One can only read between the lines and discover that they are inspired by satan, the very spirit that endowed Jezebel with mystical powers of manipulation and control.

Lucifer exalted himself but ended in total humiliation and damnation. This is what is written about him, "How you are fallen from heaven, O Lucifer, son of the morning! How you are cut down to the ground, you who weakened the nations! For you said in your heart: 'I will ascend into heaven, I will exalt my throne above the stars of God; I will also sit on the mount of the congregation, on the farthest sides of the north; I will ascend above the heights of the clouds, I will be like the Most High.' Yet you shall be brought down to Sheol, to the lowest depths of the Pit. Those who see you will gaze at you, and consider you, saying: 'Is this the man who made the earth tremble, who shook the kingdoms." (Isaiah 14:12–16)

Laws of power without submission to the authority of the Most High will eventually humiliate and destroy anyone. The history of power and seduction has an array of historical figures who ended up in disgrace and oblivion. Memories of people like Adolf Hitler, Napoleon Bonaparte, Haile Selassie I, and the Czars live in the annals of history but not in the hearts and minds of men. On the contrary, others like Moses, King David, Queen Esther, Florence Nightingale, Mahatma Gandhi, and Nelson Mandela live in the minds and hearts of men because of their humility and servant leadership.

Moses was described as the meekest man of all the men on earth in his days (Numbers 12:3), because though he was the strongest, he used his strength to lift up others, to the extent that God made known his ways to him and his acts to the children of Israel (Psalm 103:7). Anyone who knows God's ways has a sound relationship with him and the evidence of that relationship are often backed by signs and wonders. When one knows only his acts, he or she becomes a miracle seeker and watcher. Servant leaders can stand before God and mediate between God and his creation.

Moses stood before God and pleaded with him not to destroy the people of Israel when they committed a great sin and made for themselves a god of gold. Moses, prayed to God and said, "Yet now, if You will forgive their sin—but if not, I pray blot me out of Your book which You have written" (Exodus 32:31–32). Having known the ways of God, Moses demonstrated selfless power by mentoring and passing the knowledge and vision given to him by God to the next generation (Deuteronomy 31). No wonder Moses is likened to Jesus, who humbled and took upon himself our iniquity, and has given us his authority to manifest God's glory and power on earth.

Therefore, seeking power without acknowledging the source of all laws is vanity. We were created in God's image and likeness and have been given power to dominate and transform the governing systems on earth to function as those in heaven. Our goal in life should then be to seek first the kingdom of God and his righteousness and all these things, such as power, security, influence and the vast wants we strive to achieve will be added to us (Matthew 6:33).

Chapter 24

The Hallmark of Truth—
Independence and Freedom

Freedom is based on knowledge, understanding
and application of truth.

The concept of truth baffles many, even as it did Pontius Pilate, the governor of Rome during the days of Jesus. Jesus speaking to Pilate during his trial, spoke of the truth he came into the world to bear witness to, and that everyone who is of the truth hears his voice (John 18:37–38). These statements and others like, "And you shall know the truth and the truth shall make you free … or … when He, the Spirit of truth, has come, He will guide you in all truth" inspired heated debates and divided opinions among kings, political and religious leaders (John 8:32; 16:13). To this day, the debate rages on. One may wonder, what is truth, and why is it so controversial?

Truth is the purpose for the existence of a thing, the intention that can only be found in the mind of the Creator. It conveys the functioning and appropriate use of things which are made. Truth, in other words answers the life question of why things exist, the intention of the Creator and the inbuilt consequences of misuse.

Man's existence is by no means an accident on planet earth. They were designed and equipped by the Creator to dominate the world. However, when they lost their dominion mandate, the spirit of truth that revealed their purpose for existence and connected them to their source departed. As a result, they became slaves to the prince of darkness, who like all oppressors, such as tyrants and slave masters, dehumanized and promoted ignorance among subjects.

Oppressors destroy self-identity, one's purpose for existence and the destiny of the oppressed by subjecting them to physical and mental bondage or a combination of both. Any effort to set free the oppressed, either from slavery or colonization, requires the removal of both physical and mental chains. The latter is an uphill task because it necessitates reprogramming of the mind, which involves deleting and replacing old information with new uncorrupted truth.

Champions of freedom, otherwise known as freedom fighters like Mahatma Gandhi, Martin Luther King Jr. and Nelson Mandela fought for the freedom of their oppressed people but received independence. Unfortunately, the difference between independence and freedom is like day and night. Many freedom fighters, activists, political figures, and religious leaders often confuse the two and use them interchangeably. This is incorrect! Independence, a term frequently used to mean "freedom," is in fact deliverance. It is the release from the oppressor while freedom is the release from oppression. One can be released from the oppressor but still be oppressed. Independence is like removal of physical restraints from victims of oppression, yet they are mentally bankrupt to decide for themselves and take responsibility for their actions.

The oppressor knows this fact and that explains why most countries that fought for freedom were given pacts of independence. The oppressor knew the state of mind of the oppressed as a people without sufficient knowledge and skills to make the successful transition from captivity to freedom. It was only a matter of time before the oppressed came knocking at their door seeking aid or even yearning for the "good old days" when the master provided their needs for subservience. It is often said that the security of slavery is the absence of responsibility. Freedom demands responsibility, the discovery of the truth about yourself and life, which gives you the liberty to control and manage your environment.

There are many examples from biblical and political history that illustrate the similarities between independence and deliverance, which have a sharp contrast to freedom. Some of these are captured below:

Deliverance of Israel from Egypt

Israel was delivered from Egypt by the hand of a prophet but perished in the wilderness. Why? They were delivered (salvaged) but not freed. God understands that deliverance is an event, but freedom is a process, a function of what you know, not just the removal of physical chains. Hence, God's decision to take Israel into the wilderness rather than directly into the promise land.

The wilderness experience had two-fold objectives; First, God had to reiterate the universal fact that there is no freedom without the law. Laws are fundamental to every nation because they influence, build and impact culture, institutions, and communities. And that is precisely what God gave Moses, the first "prime minister" of Israel on Mount Sinai. Secondly, to purge and prune the children of Israel of the slavery mindset. This mindset manifested in the face of adversity and other challenges associated with responsibility, where they desired to return to captivity. Like many who have been delivered but not set free, the children of Israel desired to return to their comfort zones as opposed to learning and embracing the changes that came with taking full control of their destiny. This behavior resonates with many oppressed people who have been delivered from oppression but are yet to be mentally transformed.

The Church as the "Salvation Army"

The church was established to continue the kingdom's agenda to salvage mankind from the bondage of sin and transform their minds to reign again. Salvation set the pace for transformation akin to the message of God through Moses to Pharaoh,

"Let my people go!" It is not freedom but deliverance. Freedom is the knowledge, understanding and application of the truth, which transforms and frees the mind, whereas deliverance is the removal of chains from captives.

Like the children of Israel, who desired to return to Egypt, many who have been delivered but not set free from oppression still seek the benefits and comforts of the oppressor at the expense of freedom. This is evident among practicing Christians, who like freedom fighters, have confused deliverance with freedom. Many are drawn to the doctrine of deliverance, a "quick fix for heaven," whereas God wants them to be mature and rule the world.

In deliverance ministry, the emphasis is on the expulsion of oppressive or evil spirits from victims, leaving them prone to repossession by even worse spirits, because they are not taught the ways to live post deliverance (Luke 11:24-26), after which a false sense of security or peace is adopted to mask the brutal reality of self-doubt and strings of unfulfilled promises. Consequently, when things get tough with such individuals, escapism becomes the center of their prayer, "Lord, come quickly and take us home."

The Oppressed and Oppressor Syndrome

Several nations that gained their independence from colonial masters decades ago have not been able to successfully transform their minds to develop productive and sustainable economic bases. Subjection to oppression created a dependency syndrome and disempowered them from taking control of their destinies.

The legacy of oppression was built on dehumanization and is sustained by the ignorance of truth. Information is intentionally hidden from the oppressed and seeds of discord sown to destabilize, manipulate while resources are extracted from them. This explains the senseless springs of conflict in nations that were or continue to be under the influence of oppression.

Besides the corrupt ideology of colonization employed by colonial masters to extract resources, religion was used as an additional tool to destabilize traditional institutions and cultures that had existed in the colonies prior to their arrival. They brought the Bible but not the God of the Bible, and as a result, dislodged kings and kingdoms and replaced them with religious institutions that also lacked a true relationship with the Creator.

Religion does not set people free, rather it breeds division, irresponsibility, creates a spirit of dependency, resentment, and contentment, while stunting development and creativity. It has been described as the opium of people. In the words of Karl Marx, "Religion is the sigh of the oppressed creatures, the heart of a heartless world, and the soul of the soulless condition."[31]

Colonial masters developed systems to suppress their subjects while protecting their interest, because they desired to maintain their grip on the slaves. They lacked the true knowledge of the Creator and his intent for creation which caused them to pin down subjects, forgetting that both would make no advancement. In the words of Desmond Tutu, "When the missionaries came to Africa, they had the Bible and we had the land. They said, 'Let us pray.' We closed our eyes. When we opened them, we had the Bible and they had the land."[32] Surely, this cannot be what God intended for his creation.

Unlike religion, knowledge of the truth sets both the oppressor and oppressed free. Jesus recognized such traits among the religious folks in his days and rebuked them, saying, "Woe to you, scribes and Pharisees, hypocrites! For you shut up the kingdom of heaven against men; for you neither go in yourself, nor do you allow those who are entering to go in" (Matthew 23:13).

God created humans as sovereign beings with a free will to dominate the earth—the colony of heaven. God is the only "colonial master", whose colony declared independence and were enslaved as a result. In other words, they turned their backs on the truth and used the power of choice given to them to enter bondage. Subsequently, they invented religion to answer questions of identity, origin, purpose, and destiny. This search birthed virtually all the inhumane acts and atrocities we see today. Nonetheless, amid all this, at the appointed time, God sent his Son to deliver mankind from the bondage of sin.

One may wonder why after mankind was delivered more than two thousand years ago by the death of Jesus, freedom is still an illusion and not a reality. First, humans were not designed to dominate each other. That is why it is easy to put shackles on humans but difficult to unshackle the mind out of the experience. Secondly, freedom is a burden because it is not free, it has a hefty price tag that requires disposing off acquired erroneous ideologies. This explains why many people find slavery a lot easier to deal with as opposed to freedom because as a slave your master takes care of you 100 percent whereas, when dealing with freedom, it demands responsibility, adherence to the law and accountability to the state which can be very challenging for one with a truth deprived mind.

Anyone who becomes a citizen of the kingdom of heaven signs up for a steep learning curve which entails giving up old lifestyles and embracing the kingdom's culture. This process is referred to as the renewing of the mind which can prove incredibly challenging and time consuming, yet attainable (Romans 12:2; Hebrews 12:2). Citizenship in the kingdom immerses you into a culture, not a collection of rituals or religion. You can practice a religion but not citizenship. No matter where you are, what you do, you remain a citizen.

The kingdom lifestyle bears no sign. People would hardly know your citizenship until you speak. The carrier of the kingdom lifestyle lives within the citizen—the Holy Spirit (Luke 17:20–21). He has the mandate and the responsibility of transforming the lifestyle of a delivered person to that of the kingdom (Ephesians 4:23-24). He does not control, manipulate or coax one to change but only helps them by offering godly council and guidance. Therefore, we have the choice to accept and cooperate with him or not. The world is watching us, and because of us, they will decide what they think of the King and his kingdom.

Representing your country is a part of your civic and corporate duty. So, when you take the constitution out of context or read into it rather than reading out of it, you miss your rights and privileges. In that regard, for one to be truly free, they need to have the right information, understanding and appropriate skills. Furthermore, they need to take full responsibility of judging their sources of information so they can discern truth from facts, right from wrong and good from bad.

Reading and understanding the Word of God gives one legal power. A person who knows and understands truth cannot be manipulated. Like Jesus, who despite being God, studied the word, grew in wisdom and was able to discern the manipulation of the Scriptures by the devil. He immersed himself in the written Word of God and the Spirit brought the right words to his mind when he needed them. This gave no room for misinterpretations and accusations from both man (religious leaders) and the devil (Acts 13:28; John 14:30).

The Word of God should not be interpreted through pre-existing concepts, because some of them have been influenced and contaminated by seminary teachings, pastors, songs and sunday school lessons. The King anticipated this problem and provided an expert counselor to us, the Holy Spirit, who can personally help us recapture the essence of the word that came from the mind of God (John 16:13). Without the Holy Spirit, we superimpose our concepts from our culture and environment onto God's Word (Colossians 2:8). We then proceed to build our lives on the conclusions that we have derived from reading into the Bible, instead of reading out of it and often than not, run into error.

Paul the apostle commended the Berean church for their noble-mindedness, "In that they received the word with all readiness, and searched the Scriptures daily to find out whether these things were so" (Acts 17:11). They were not gullible believers; they went after the truth just as Paul had written and urged Timothy saying, "Be diligent to present yourself approved to God, a worker who does not need to be ashamed, rightly dividing the word of truth" (2 Timothy 2:15). Sir Francis Bacon, published the famous phrase, "Knowledge is power."[33] In the context of this write-up, the phrase can be recast as, "Knowledge of the truth is power." Knowledge of the truth that you are a son and not a servant of God changes the dynamics of our relationship with the king and his kingdom government.

In the Old Testament, God called his people, my servants, because they had to serve him and obey all the laws of Moses and the prophets to get a recompense. They had to perform to receive. Servanthood in the old dispensation was a funda-mental concept as we read in the books of Exodus, Job and Amos: "Let my people go that they may serve me in the wilder-ness" (Exodus 7:16). "If they obey and serve Him, they shall spend their days in prosperity, and their years in pleasures" (Job 36:11). "Have you considered My servant Job, that there is none like him on the earth" (Job 2:3). "Surely the Lord God does nothing, unless he reveals His secret to his servants the prophets" (Amos 3:7).

Contrary to the old covenant, in the new covenant God refers to those who believe in Jesus whom he sent as sons (John 6:29; Galatians 3:26). In this covenant, sonship is a cardinal principle. The knowledge and understanding of this principle of sonship makes you free, even as it is written, "Therefore if the Son makes you free, you shall be free indeed" (John 8:36).

At the fall, mankind declared independence from their home country and became subjects to an illegal authority. They lost their self-identity, divine rights, privileges, mastery of circumstances and the freedom to determine their destiny. Like Moses, who delivered the nation of Israel into the wilderness to receive and live by God's law or perish, Jesus delivered us and has given us the Holy Spirit to reveal and transform our minds to conform to God's Word. This word is the truth that underpins our freedom because there is no freedom without the knowledge of the truth and obedience to the law.

God, by his Son and Spirit, returned mankind's authority over the colony. He is, therefore, the only king who extended his kingdom to a distant colony, lost it, and purposed to restore it to its original state after it declared independence. Understanding God's restoration agenda and our roles as sons, is the hallmark of truth for believers who as ambassadors of Christ are expected to have the mind of God in order to implement heaven's policies on earth and make it function like heaven.

Chapter 25

Freedom from Religion and Humanism in the 21st century

In previous chapters, we discovered that freedom is a function of the truth one knows, understands, and applies. Religion, on the other hand is the search by mankind for a deity and the pursuit of power to control circumstances. We also established that the Bible is not a religious book and its message is not about a religion. It is a kingdom book, whose message is about a king, his domain, and his governing authority. We also noted that the Creator, as King of the universe, decided to extend his governing authority from the invisible to the visible realm to be governed by his royal family—humankind.

Adam and Eve were the first legitimate authority in the colony whose headquarters was the garden of Eden. From Eden, the human family was expected to multiply and spread into all the earth as one people under one God with one language. God, the source, and lord of the universe was the ultimate authority in the home country—heaven. He delegated authority over the earth—the colony of heaven— to our first parents. When they disobeyed him, they lost their divine right to govern the colony. At that point, the Spirit of God that dwelled in them and gave them divine direction, akin to our modern-day GPS, returned to the home country. In other words, they went "off the grid."

Consequently, they were expelled from the garden of Eden and stepped into uncharted territory and the rules of the jungle kicked in. Such rules inspired irresponsibility, jealousy, murder, and all manner of ungodliness. Nonetheless, their will to survive was not deterred. After long years of wandering, they and their descendants perceived the danger of losing the unity of their race and decided to take their destiny into their hands. They said to themselves, "Come let us build ourselves a city, and a tower whose top is in the heavens; let us make a name for ourselves, lest we be scattered abroad over the face of the whole earth" (Genesis 11:1–9).

The story continues that God confused their language and scattered them abroad over the face of the earth. This event took place in the land of Shinar and the tower was called Babel. The motive to build a city and a tower whose top was in the heavens was humankind's attempt to conquer the earth and the heavens and make themselves gods. This was the birth of the ideology of humans taking divine and natural laws into their hands in the attempt to be their own god.

As they were scattered over all the earth, they divided themselves into various nations according to their different languages and built cities for themselves. Humanity lost their oneness as a people and established the kingdoms of the earth (Psalm 2:1–2). These kingdoms were called Gentile nations and were under the authority of the god of this world, satan—the prince of darkness.

When God decided to implement his alternate plan to re-colonize the earth, he found and called a man named Abraham and through his seed, the nation of Israel was established to serve as a prototype for God's recolonization program. Israel became the first nation on earth that believed in one God unlike the other nations (Gentiles). The recolonization program would serve as a platform for God to re-establish himself as king over all the earth. The restoration of the heavenly government and divine kingship on earth would be laid upon the shoulder of Jesus the Seed of a woman—Mary, who was a descendant of Abraham (Isaiah 9:6).

Israel was expected to be one nation under one God—Yahweh, but they disregarded the script and wanted to be like other nations with earthly kings. That is where the history of kings in Israel began with the enthronement of king Saul as their first king (1 Samuel 9:27; 10:1). God never wanted Israel to have an earthly king like other Gentile nations (1 Samuel 8:5–7). He wanted to be their King, Lawgiver and Judge, who embodied the three arms of government— executive, legislative and judiciary (Isaiah 33:22). Israel rejected God as king and eventually adopted the religious ways of worship practiced by fallen nations.

God never gave anyone a religion, be it to Adam and Eve, Abraham, Moses, or any other prophet and neither did Jesus establish one. God always wanted a relationship with his royal family. Jesus faced the rudest and cruelest opposition from the religious leaders, the Pharisees, Sadducees and scribes whose focus was religion rather than empowering the children of Israel to know and have a relationship with God.

Religion was established by fallen nations who were searching for what our first parents lost—a divine governing authority to dominate the earth and the systems upon it. The fundamental practices of religion are rituals characterized by highly formal ceremonies like sacrifices, offerings, processions, and methods of divination. In many religious sects, people are held captive by rituals, traditions or invent ways to worship all manner of idols as a means of finding favor and blessings with "God" (Mark 7:1–23; Colossians 2:8). The inspiration to have and worship other gods was the handiwork of the fallen angel, the deceptive dragon called Lucifer. Lucifer wanted to be God and be worshiped. When he lost the battle in heaven and was thrown to the earth, he orchestrated the fall of mankind and cunningly set himself as the ultimate idol to be worshiped. By such maneuvers, he ruled the kingdoms of the earth and continues to blind those who are unaware of his defeat more than two thousand years ago (Luke 4:5–7; 2 Corinthians 4:4).

As mentioned earlier, God never gave Israel a religion but the Torah—the law of God revealed to Moses and recorded in the five books of the scriptures, purposed to guide the people.

When God called Abraham, he promised to give him and his descendants a land flowing with milk and honey, not a religion. That explains why the first thing God gave Israel once they were delivered from slavery in Egypt, was the Ten Commandments not a religion. They were to live by God's laws and commandments and have no other god but him. While Israel had Yahweh as their only God, the rest of the nations continued with their ritualistic worship of idols. The earth therefore had two groups of nations, Jews and Gentiles, separated by their belief systems.

As the years went by, free thinkers and writers emerged from the Gentile nations among whom were people who did not believe in God (atheists) and those who doubted his existence (agnostics). They worshiped neither God nor idols and embraced the love of wisdom, a philosophy that began in Greece and reached its heights in the works of Plato and Aristotle. These irreligious groups have not relented their efforts to be free from any notion of a god or religion. The establishment of organizations such as, Freedom from Religion, are movements of thinkers, atheists, and agnostics, who believe in the self-existence of humankind—a spice of humanism.

Though atheists, agnostics and other philosophers did not constitute themselves into a nation, they successfully infiltrated both Jewish and Gentile nations with their teachings and influenced their beliefs and governing systems with their ideologies. Israel, unlike the Gentiles, has been the target for annihilation, because of their calling to usher the divine plan of God on earth. Satan fought Abraham and his descendants at every twist and turn, and finally cornered them in Egypt. Even after God delivered them by the hand of Moses, they murmured against him and wandered in the wilderness for forty years. The nation of Israel in the wilderness was a foreshadow of the New Testament congregation—the church of Jesus Christ (Acts 7:37–38). Like Israel in the desert, the church has not focused on its assignment to make the earth function like heaven but complain about how tough the world is and then pray to escape from it to heaven.

Ecclesia in classical Greek was a term used to describe political gatherings of citizens for the purpose of conducting the affairs of the state. Jesus established his own ecclesia, called the church, as an assembly of citizens of the kingdom with the mandate to preach the good news of the returned heavenly governing authority to the earth. Hence, the church is not a religious organization searching for God, but a political entity established by him and commissioned by Jesus to restore his authority on the earth.

This sets apart the church from religion and addresses the claims made by organizations that lobby for separation of church and state such as the "freedom from religion" movement. The ideology of the Freedom from Religion Foundation that promotes the separation of church and state would better read as "separation of state from religion." Furthermore, the account by Thomas Jefferson referred to as the separation of state from the church should rather be viewed as a separation of government from religion. The church is a political system with ambassadors who represent the king's agenda on the earth. The original intention for the establishment of the church was to inspire earthly governments to have policies, constitutions and laws that are aligned with the will of God. In that regard, every government on earth was expected to take its cue from the political assembly of the king of the universe. Unfortunately, this is not the case.

The misconception of church as a religion and the notion of Christianity to mean followers of Christ are incorrect and need clarification. The church is an assembly of citizens of the kingdom of heaven commissioned by Jesus to represent him on earth while he is in heaven. Paul rightly referred to the followers of Jesus as ambassadors for Christ, not Christians (2 Corinthians 5:20). Christianity was a derogatory term used by pagans in Antioch to ascribe a religion to a people who were not worshiping their idol gods but Jesus (Acts 11:26). Hence, Christianity became a religion and their buildings and prem-ises where people congregated were referred to as church. As Christianity became a religion and the church a religious or-ganization, Jesus was then perceived as the spiritual leader of Christians, just as Moses was to Judaism, Mohammad to Islam and Buddha to Buddhism.

Religion has caused more pain, suffering and death to hu-manity than all other wars put together. Numerous atrocities have been committed in the name of God by religious fanatics. Religious savagery and confusion justified the call by many statesmen to advocate for the separation of state and reli-gion. States should be secular (irreligious). In a secular state or country, religion does not inspire, nor does it play a part in law making. Its laws are not based on religion or cite an official religion, the state is kept separate from religion, and the state does not discriminate nor favor persons based on their religious beliefs. Within a secular state, the government does not interfere with religion and its activities, as long as such activities are done under the confines of the law. The establishment of a secular state is necessary if a country is to have true freedom from religion. Countries can become secular states upon creation, or after undergoing secularization where religion is separated from the state.

In that regard, a state can be secular under one God. It does not have an established state religion or an equivalent. The debate on state and religion could have been the motivation for Thomas Jefferson's call for a "wall of separation between church and state."[34] But it became murky when Jefferson perceived the church as a religion. The idea of separation of church and state is actually not part of the U.S. Constitution and the First Amendment to the Constitution states that "Congress shall make no law respecting an establishment of religion or prohibiting the free exercise thereof…"[35] Hence it ensures the religious freedom of U.S. citizens and maintains its stand as a secular nation under one God as written in the official motto of the nation, "In God We Trust."[36]

The report of the American president weighing in on the American peoples' religious right to pray in schools and public places[37] raises some eyebrows. Prayer is a divine human right and not a religious activity. Surprisingly, many evangelicals who came to the President's defense were directly or indirectly referring to their constituencies as religious organizations rather than assemblies of ambassadors for Christ. The president, in a sense, was standing for all religious rights that would include "Christianity," Islam Judaism, Buddhism, Hinduism etc.

There is no doubt religion and religious studies in schools have done lots of good to tame our morals and keep humanity searching for their identity, purpose, and source. However, that alone cannot set us free. Freedom from religion can only be realized by accepting the lordship of Jesus and the governing authority he brought. With that in mind, every state government is supposed to be free from the influence of religious institutions. The ideal position for a government is to establish institutions that teach kingdom government and civic responsibility as a divine right to all citizens.

Wisdom demands that states and citizenry should acknowledge the ills of religious conflicts and make it clear that the state is irreligious but recognizes the Creator as king of the universe and work toward justice, equality and peace for all. Otherwise, religious confusion, hatred, destruction, and killings in the name of 'God' will continue. The ideology that fans religious terrorism is well documented. Blaise Pascal wrote these words: "The concept of a just or holy war is an ancient one. The Jews used the concept, and it was probably from them that Christians and Muslims adopted it. All three principal monotheistic religions still accept the idea and continue to use it. For Jews it is a kherem, for Muslims it is a jihad, and for Christians a crusade."[38]

Fighting and killing one another in the name of God represents ignorance of the highest degree. It is evil, underpinned by a religious conviction and dead conscience. Pascal succinctly captured it this way; "Men never do evil so completely and cheerfully as when they do it from religious conviction."[39] And Jesus, referring to the same degree of ignorance, on numerous occasions rebuked the teachers of the law for inspiring religious hierarchy and sectarianism among the people, thus misrepresenting the kingdom of God.

If God is almighty, he should be able to defend himself and his creation, not the other way round. Claiming to be a Christian warrior or a jihadist is misguided. God has a kingdom with citizens, a constitution, and an army to defend his domain including the inhabitants in the colony. When war broke out in heaven, God never fought! His army of angels fought on his behalf. As Lord of hosts and God of order, he has constituencies that undertake different tasks. His angels also watch over and defend the colony and its citizens. Fighting with swords against flesh and blood was an Old Testament phenomenon because the colony rebelled against the home country and became defenseless, and as a result, the kings of the earth trained warriors to protect their domains. Otherwise, from creation it was not supposed to be so. There is no account of our first parents fighting to defend God or themselves while in Eden and this is the position Jesus restored humankind to. This is the good news of the kingdom of heaven returning to the earth. It is not good news of a religion with members who are still searching for God, the search ended more than two thousand years ago.

The effects of religion are unfolding before our eyes. The search for "god" has culminated into a "new humanism" as it was at the tower of Babel. This philosophy is rejecting the authority and kingship of God and the gospel of the return of the government of heaven on earth, with the intention to create a one-world religion and government. In this system, the one world religion places mankind at the center of the new government and not Christ.[40] Thus humanizing God; instead of us doing his will, we have invented our own wills to the extent that, "We are our own gods and our own devil."[41]

Humanism is not a new phenomenon. It began when humankind declared independence from the home country and attempted to build the tower that would reach the heavens, a foreshadow of the 21st century agenda of a new humanism, one-world religion and government. The intended deal of the 21st century Babel is expected to be cemented in the Vatican before the end of the year 2020. A statement about this reads, "In a renewed and enthusiastic endorsement of globalism, Pope Francis has announced he is hosting an initiative for a "Global Pact" to create a "new humanism."[42] The theme of the initiative, "Re-inventing the Global Educational Alliance" has a hidden agenda. One may wonder, why education? Because God will be removed from educational systems and replaced with humanist ethics. Not surprising, in the year 2010, the godless United Nations produced a text, a first contribution to

UNESCO's reflection on a new humanism captioned, "A New Humanism for the 21st Century."[43]

In a write-up on a New Approach to the Humanist Philosophy and Humanist Ethics, Carl Coon wrote, "God, at least the God we used to worship, can now be recognized as a device of the human imagination. Morality, it follows, is equally a human invention. Common sense must replace the Scriptures and the priesthood as the validator of our moral code. And why not? Part of the modern humanist ethic is the core belief that humanity, not some imagined deity, is ultimately responsible for our common fate and future." Coon, further argues that, "In our time, as a new humanist spirit slowly infiltrates and supplants old-fashioned theism, modern ethical structures are gradually altering the moral precepts that were codified by the old religions and sanctioned by the common sense of bygone generations."[44]

Corliss Lamont, in his book, The Philosophy of Humanism also had this to say, "For his great achievements man, utilizing the resources and the laws of Nature, yet without Divine aid, can take full credit. Similarly, for his shortcomings he must take full responsibility. Humanism assigns to man nothing less than the task of being his own savior and redeemer."[45]

The philosophy of humanism that places mankind as their own savior and redeemer, coupled with religious confusion are leading humanity into uncharted territory. The pope has been canvassing other religious world leaders for the establishment of a one-world religion. Plans to host the Global Pact to create a new humanism initiative will culminate into a marriage between religion and humanism to form a one-world government. The old humanism school of thought held the view that, humans were social animals for millions of years before becoming intellectual beings. Upon attaining their intellectual self-consciousness, they turned the social rules and norms into religion and morality. The philosophy stopped short of calling humankind evolving gods. This is exactly what the new humanism movement is bent on doing, that is, declaring that mankind is their own god and can govern themselves without any supernatural intervention.

In another twist, Cardinal Raymond Burke said, "The Vatican's global pact for 'new humanism' promotes one-world government, opposes Christ's Kingship and is an effort to dull people's consciousness about the Kingship of Our Lord Jesus Christ as it is proclaimed in the Gospel."[46] Burke criticized the notion of a one-world government by saying, "The idea of a one-world government is fundamentally the same phenomenon that was displayed by the builders of the Tower of Babel who presumed to exercise the power of God on earth to unite heaven with earth, which is simply incorrect."[47]

In the years to come, the world will witness the effects of placing the human at the center of life instead of Christ. It is no coincidence the Global Pact Initiative would take place in Europe. The golden image in king Nebuchadnezzar's dream offers insight regarding the establishment of the one-world government and its demise. In the dream, the king saw an image with a head of gold, chest and arms of silver, belly and thighs of bronze, legs of iron and its feet of iron and clay

(Daniel 2:31–35). The head of gold symbolized the Babylonian Empire under Nebuchadnezzar; the chest and arms of silver represented the Medo-Persian Empire under Darius and Cyrus; the belly and thighs represented the Greek Empire under Alexander; the legs of iron symbolized the Roman Empire under Caesar; and its feet of iron and clay epitomized the reunion of European nations under the anti-Christ.

Daniel revealed the fate of the image to the king, saying, "You watched while a stone was cut out without hands, which struck the image on its feet of iron and clay, and broke them into pieces...And the stone that struck the image became a great mountain and filled the whole earth" (Daniel 2:34–35). Clay and iron do not mix easily, so has been the struggle to keep the European Union together. The Global Pact on the "New Humanism" in Rome will promote the one-world government and set the stage for the emergence of the anti-Christ. But Christ, the Chief Cornerstone will crush the system and establish an everlasting kingdom government that will fill the whole earth.

The season of reckoning is at hand, whose report will you believe: that of the kings, political and religious leaders of the earth or the report of the coming King of Kings and Lord of Lords from the kingdom of heaven?

Chapter 26

Kingdom Sovereignty and Stewardship

G od is the source of all things, the king of the universe and Lord of the earth by virtue of creation. He gave man the legal authority to steward all things on the earth on his behalf. By implication, man is tasked with the management of the earth which involves cultivating, protecting and supervising God's resources. Should anything happen on earth, good or bad, man is entirely responsible. God can only intervene when called upon by man and should he desire to do anything on earth, he would first consult with man for permission.

At various times, God consulted with man to have his will done on the earth. Some of these events include; when he wanted to destroy Sodom and Gomorrah for sexual perversion, dialogued with Abraham to allow him; and the Lord said, "Shall I hide from Abraham what I am doing?" (Genesis 18:17). When he had to deliver Israel after they cried unto him from their agony in Egypt, he sent a man called Moses. And he said, "Now therefore, behold, the cry of the children of Israel has come to Me, and I have also seen the oppression with which the Egyptians oppress them. Come now, therefore, and I will send you to Pharaoh that you may bring My people, the children of Israel, out of Egypt" (Exodus 3:9–10). There were multiple instances where God had to speak to man to get things done but the ultimate event occurred when God wanted to save the world, he gave his Son, as it is written, "For God so loved the world that he gave His only begotten Son, that whoever believes in him should not perish but have everlasting life" (John 3:16).

God values his word, and that explains why he never intervenes on the earth without man's consent. Though he is God, owner of the heavens and the earth and his presence and influence span from the invisible to the visible realms, he respects man's sovereignty over the earth. He is love and created mankind in his image and likeness and entrusted them with the sovereign rule over the earth and all therein. The sovereignty he gave his royal family was not that of ownership but of stewardship, a management contract as referenced in scriptures, "The heaven, even the heavens are the Lord's but the earth He has given to the children of men" (Psalm 115:16).

The infinite knowledge of the Creator spans 360 degrees from the north, through east, south, west and back to the north where he has established his throne (Psalm 48:2; Isaiah 46:9–10; 42:9). We, humans have limited knowledge and have struggled over the years to increase our intellectual base.

Many have acquired bachelor's degrees, some master's and others PhDs, just three degrees compared with God's 360 degrees. The cream of our society prides themselves in the acquisition of intellectual knowledge and scholastic certificates. Only a return to our divine nature can enable mankind to close the 357-degree gap. Jesus had 360-degree knowledge and is called the greatest physician, philosopher, and theologian that ever walked planet earth. He was raised by a carpenter and grew up in a small unknown town called Nazareth. His secret to success was a total dependence on God's Word and Spirit (Luke 2:52).

In The Incomparable *Christ*, Tim Challies described Jesus as a man born contrary to the laws of life, who in infancy startled a king, in childhood puzzled doctors and as a man ruled the course of nature. His enemies could not destroy him, neither could the grave hold him. He conquered death and reigns as Lord and Savior of all humanity[48].

Candidly, in a song by Voice of the Cross[49], the question is asked, "What Manner of Man Is Jesus?" Jesus was indeed a wonder. At age twelve he knew who he was and when he was asked by his parents who were searching for him, he said, "Why do you seek Me? Did you not know that I must be about My father's business?" (Luke 2:49). For the next eighteen years, all that is known about his life is summarized thus: "And Jesus increased in wisdom and stature, and in favor with God and men" (Luke 2:52). By age thirty, his only agenda was to do the work of his Father. He said to his disciples, "My food is to do the will of Him who sent Me and to finish his work"

(John 4:34). When distraction showed up in the garden of Gethsemane, he bowed his will to his Father's, saying, "Nevertheless, not what I will but what You will" (Mark 14:36). This is the apex of stewardship.

Many gifted men and women, in their lifetimes, have turned out to be byproducts or proverbs of their generation, because they never submitted their gifts to the "Giver of gifts" and when the enemy rose up against them, they crumbled like stacks of cards. Like our first parents, many continue to fail the stewardship assignment. But God in his infinite mercies staged a comeback to restore man's sovereignty over the earth. The choice to walk in that sovereignty remains solely in the hands of mankind.

God respects our choices. When he is dealing with us and our stewardship responsibilities, he allows us to exercise our free will to choose between good and evil, life and death, else we become compelled like robots and can blame him for whatever happens. We have the power of choice to be a Joseph or a Samson; a Jacob or Esau; a Peter or a Judas. These figures all faced the stewardship and character test and each one of them responded differently. Joseph refused and run away when his master's wife wanted to drag him into sexual immorality (Genesis 39:7–9), and as a result preserved his destiny. Samson on the other hand bowed to Delilah's seduction and lost his authority and power as judge of Israel (Judges 16:16–17). Esau despised his birthright and sold it for a morsel of food, an action that later would cost him his Father's eternal blessings (Genesis 25:34; 27:37). Judas Iscariot betrayed Jesus for 30 pieces of silver, and instead of repenting and asking the Lord to restore him, hanged himself (Matthew 26:14–16; 27:5). Peter, however, denied Jesus but was restored when he repented and confessed his love for the master (John 18:25–27; 21:15).

To safeguard our stewardship mandate, God made two wills for himself to protect his integrity and secure his ultimate purpose for creation. His perfect will to ensure he gets what he purposed at the beginning of creation and a passive will to accommodate the changes in his plans that are as a result of man's will.

Examples of God's passive will are shown clearly in his dealings with pompous kings and nations in biblical history. When Israel forgot about him, while in Egypt, God raised up Pharaoh to oppress them (Exodus 9:16). This awakened them to call upon God for a deliverer. He then sent Moses who led the children of Israel across the wilderness. When Israel wanted an earthly king as other fallen nations, and said to Samuel, "Now make us a king to judge us like all the nations" (1 Samuel 8:5), God passively allowed and directed Samuel to anoint Saul as King of Israel, saying, "Heed the voice of the people in all that they say to you; for they have not rejected you, but have rejected Me, that I should not reign over them" (v. 7). God spelled out the consequences of their rejection of him as their King and opting for a man (v. 18), and they paid a heavy price for their choice. Even with their wrong choice, God was gracious to let them have a glimpse of the king, Jesus whom he had prepared for Israel and the Gentile nations, through the prototype kingdom of King David.

David and his reign was the shadow of the kingdom government Jesus would bring on his shoulder, which is evidently captured in the Bible saying, "Of the increase of His government and peace there will be no end, upon the throne of David and over His kingdom, to order it and establish it with judgement and justice from that time forward, even forever" (Isaiah 9:7). Like David, the obscure shepherd boy with no charisma before his father and prophet Samuel, so was Jesus, born in a manger and rejected by the Jewish priests and people, who cried out, "Away with Him, away with Him! Crucify Him! Pilate said to them, shall I crucify your King? The chief priests answered, we have no king but Caesar!" (John 19:15). And the people answered and said, "His blood be on us and on our children" (Matthew 27:25). They evoked a generational curse. Even to this day, blood has continued to flow in the land.

Nations and ethnic groups are established by God, as it is written, "And He has made from one blood every nation of men to dwell on all the face of the earth, and has determined their pre-appointed times and the boundaries for their dwellings, so that they should seek the Lord, in that they might reach out for Him and find Him, though He is not far away from each one of us, ... For we are also his offspring" (Acts 17:26–28). Even though God created us and established us in different ethnic groups he allows us the choice to seek him. Therefore, we need to be the spring that stays connected to the source.

Looking down history lanes, as at the time of the construction of the tower of Babel, man sought to go against the will of God and were scattered, as a result different ethnic groups were established throughout the earth. God continues to deal with nations and ethnic groups that rebel against his principles and established leadership in four major ways; First, he allows them to be taken into captivity (2 Kings 17:5–23); secondly, he allows foreigners to take over their land and rule over them (Deuteronomy 28:43–53); thirdly, he allows locusts to ravage the land (v. 42); and fourthly, he allows evil leaders to rise up and bring terror upon the citizens (Exodus 9:16). We have a choice to make—to understand why we should obey God and to submit to his ordinance as God and Lord over our nations, as it is written, "Blessed is the nation whose God is the Lord, the people He has chosen as His inheritance" (Psalm 33:12).

Scriptures caution all citizen to obey all governing authority; for there is no authority except that which is appointed by God (Romans 13:1). "Therefore submit yourselves to every institution of man for the Lord's sake, whether to the king as supreme or to governors, as to those who are sent by him for the punishment of evildoers and for the praise of those who do good" (1 Peter 2:13–14). There is no room for disobedience or rebellion against authority. If you are dissatisfied with any leadership institution, seek God who appointed them and request him for change. He has the power to cause leaders in authority to change their ways or remove them entirely. The heart of those in authority is in the hands of the Lord, as it is written, "The Kings heart is in the hand of the

Lord, like the rivers of water; He turns it wherever He wishes" (Proverbs 21:1).

It is often said that God gives a people the leadership they deserve, and leaders reflect the people—an accurate overview of the history of Israel, as narrated in Psalm 106. Israel rejected God repeatedly and God allowed them to follow their own lusts. They did not want to be a peculiar people with God as their King. They wanted to be like other nations when they asked for a king and God gave them Saul and the consequences were severe.

Rebellion is not a viable option or remedy for injustice, because God equates it to the sin of witchcraft (1 Samuel 15:23). Just because something seems good does not make it right. Invoking God's will and dealing with the root cause of bad leadership and government is the best option. The appalling state of families, communities, and nations that have embraced civil disobedience and rebellion against leadership fill-up pages of history.

The storms of life are used by God as wake up calls for humanity to make choices. In most cases, storms of life can be perceived as divine "knockouts" to enable us to recalibrate our course. Though the storms may come, and divine encounters sent our way, God will always respect our choices. The father never refused giving the prodigal son his inheritance when he asked for it and never went in search of him to bring him back home. The prodigal son had an epiphany and decided to return home to his father. God never stopped the children of Israel when they decided to make a golden calf at the foot of Mount Sinai when Moses delayed on the mountain. Neither did he stop Eve from being deceived by the serpent nor Adam from rebelling against his word by eating the fruit his wife presented to him. They all had choices, and God respected them.

Regardless of our choices, God has made available to us a helper who is the Holy Spirit, our divine GPS who re-routes us unto the right path. Challenges, trials and even temptations are "necessary evils" in our lives. We have the choice to listen, seek and obey the helper because the choices we make have inherent rewards or consequences. Moses thought it was justified for him to kill the Egyptian to free his Israeli brother, but his error earned him 40 years as a shepherd boy in Midian until the burning bush experience re-routed him back into his deliverance mission. Jacob, the deceiver, conned his elder brother of his blessing, even though he had a special future. Thereafter, he lived in fear of his brother's reproach and had to wrestle with God's angel to reclaim his destiny as father of the nation of Israel. Saul, the persecutor of the followers of Jesus, thought he was doing God a favor by ridding off a group of blasphemers, until he was knocked off his horse, and became Paul the apostle to the Gentiles.

As sovereign beings and stewards of God's resources on earth, we are to demonstrate responsible leadership by:

- ➤ Accepting God's final sacrifice for sin and his finished work for humanity.
- ➤ Obeying God and enjoying the free gift of grace.

- ➤ Speaking victory over failure and blessings over curses.
- ➤ Acting on God's Word and committing all our ways unto God for divine guidance.
- ➤ Making plans and submitting them to the Master planner who provides the resources for us to execute the plans.
- ➤ Respecting authority, pursuing honest gains and serving others.

What we believe in is fundamental because all things are done according to our faith. Our faith is a function of our belief system. As stewards, God never coaxes our choices. He only gives us what we ask, need, and believe for, according to his will. The woman with the flow of blood heard about Jesus' healing power, believed it, and acted by pushing her way through the crowd to touch the border of the Master's garment and received healing (Luke 8:43–48). You and I have the power to choose what we hear, watch, read, meditate on, believe in, and finally act upon because these aspects influence and impact our sovereign authority over the earth.

The stewardship mandate is therefore that of management and not ownership. It demands accountability and obedience to God as our source and sustainer. With the power of choice that we possess, we need to examine potential consequences before taking any decisions, because consequences are more important than decisions and linger long after the decisions have been made.

Our stewardship responsibility is dependent on the decisions we make; hence we should withhold all decisions until we fully understand their effects on us and others. Even after considering the effects, we should continue to petition or ask God to order our footsteps (Psalm 37:23).

Chapter 27

God's Ways and Our Choices

God's ways are guided by principles hidden in biblical stories and parables. The stories in the Old Testament have hidden principles, whereas the New Testament contains parables that reveal the principles. Principles are fundamental laws on which everything stands. They never change. When we learn the principles of things, we are always protected by them.

Facts, on the other hand, are the present state of things. Unlike principles facts change. No matter what you are going through stick with the principle, because when you live by principles, facts will not bother you because you are certain that change will surely come. Dr. Myles Munroe lived and taught principles that are still speaking after he passed away in November 2014.

Get the principles of life, and nature will obey you. Whatever you compromise to get, you will lose. Never reduce your value for an immediate experience or take a permanent decision on a temporary situation, For example, Esau despising his birthright and sold it to Jacob to satisfy his hunger (Genesis 25:34), premarital sex or bribing to get something quickly are all temporary but with lasting effects (2 Corinthians 4:18).

Humans are the only creatures that believe they can disobey principles and escape the consequences. Nonetheless, God has set principles to fix our shortcomings. These principles are intended to return, renew, recover, redeem, and restore all that was lost to its original glory.

Jesus revealed the principles hidden in the Old Testament by expounding to his disciples that beginning at Moses and the prophets, all the Scriptures were about things concerning himself (Luke 24:27). The laws of Moses prepared the people, while the prophets announced the king's coming. In the New Testament, when the king Jesus appeared on the scene, he announced his political agenda and the purpose for which he was born king—to preach the kingdom and commission the church to convey his message to all the nations of the world.

Humans are under the obligation to obey both spiritual and natural principles. Life on earth obeys the seed principle, whereby every seed has an inherent potential to germinate into a fruit tree if it is planted in the right environment. Everyone comes into the planet earth with a predestined future that is often blurred by the facts of life. Moses was born with a predestined future, to be a deliverer, but the facts of life almost distracted him. He took the law into his hands and murdered an Egyptian instead of waiting on God and suffered the consequences by spending forty years in the desert before returning to deliver Israel from bondage (Exodus 2:11–15; Hebrews 11:24–25).

Many people have dreams, but facts deter them from stepping out. Pseudo or incorrect principles that are not in line with God's will bring destruction. For examples gangs and cults have rules but these rules go against God's principles. Like a pilot, if you know your principles, you will keep your bearings and stay on course no matter the weather.

Principles are God's nature. They always supersede human culture and apply to everyone's situation, rich or poor, rule or ruled. Principles cannot be reformulated by society or enacted by parliament. For instance, God created them male and female, put in them the inherent capacity to reproduce and now we want to pervert this principle. Legislating perversion and calling it principle does not alter God's signature as seen in the male and female anatomy which we are trying to alter and abuse.

Should we so desperately need a change, we should start by establishing our own principles, formulating the appropriate nomenclatures, and be prepared for the consequences. Many nations are destroying the fabric of society, the family by promulgating laws that are against natural and spiritual principles.

God in his perfect will created man, male and female but the choice to become husband and wife, in holy matrimony, was made by Adam when he declared the first marriage in the garden of Eden, saying, "This is now bone of my bones and flesh of my flesh; She shall be called Woman, because she was taken out of Man. Therefore a man shall leave his father and mother and be joined to his wife and they shall become one flesh" (Genesis 2:23–24). God respected his choice and endorsed the declaration he had made.

When trouble struck in Eden and God questioned the man, he responded by saying, "The woman whom you gave to be with me, she gave me of the tree, and I ate" (Genesis 3:12). God was blamed for bringing the woman into Adam's life. The wise King Solomon, 'champion of many women', cautions every man to find his own wife, saying, "He who finds a wife finds a good thing, and obtains favor from the Lord" (Proverbs 18:22). It is a man's responsibility to find a wife, and not just any girl. This means she, the girl, must be committed to the lordship of Jesus, who is the bridegroom of the church. It is in God's presence that they should find one another (2 Corinthians 6:14).

God only guides the male to find a good wife and obtain favor. He does not choose a spouse but orders the footsteps of a good man to find a wife, and a woman to identify the husband with whom she will share a common vision. You can now figure out the diabolic agenda of those prophesying that sister so and so is your wife and brother so and so is your husband, because it goes against the very nature of God (2 Thessalonians 2:11).

God has not left us in the dark on what to do when we have made wrong choices. He has made us to know that all things— good or bad, work together for good to those who love him, to those who are called according to his purpose. (Romans 8:28).

God knows how to turn a mess into a message. Just stick with him and the process, and eventually you will bear good fruits (John 15:4–5) as follows:

> Adam sinned deliberately (Genesis 3:6) unlike Eve, who was deceived (v. 4). Instead of taking responsibility for his actions, he blamed God and the woman (v. 12). However, God still made provision for them outside his presence and promised to restore the dominion mandate they had lost (Genesis 3:15, 21).

> Cain killed his brother Abel and would not even accept the fact, he arrogantly asked God, "Am I my brother's keeper?" (Genesis 4:3–10). Despite that, God still set a mark of protection on Cain when he cried out to him (v. 15).

> David sinned when he committed adultery. However, he did not put the blame on Bathsheba for tempting him, nor his rooftop for exposing him to lust but confessed, "I have sinned against the Lord" (2 Samuel 12:13). And the Lord forgave him and prospered his reign over Israel.

> Paul the apostle made no excuses when Jesus confronted him for persecuting the church. Instead, he said, "Lord, what do you want me to do?" (Acts 9:6). Paul went on to become an apostle to the Gentiles and documented the lifestyle of believers in the new dispensation.

> Rev. Marcus Lamb of Daystar Television appeared before a worldwide television audience to admit he had

an affair with a woman years back and responded to three extortionists who were trying to take their pain and turn it to their gain. He said, "We're not going to take God's money to keep from being humiliated."[50] Today, Daystar Television Network is reaching out to many nations with the gospel of Jesus Christ.

➤ Sarah Jakes, a daughter of a megachurch pastor, took full responsibility for her unintended pregnancy at fourteen years, never blaming anyone for her mistake. Instead she narrated her defining moments in the book Lost & Found[51] to encourage other teenage mothers.

When we fall into temptation instead of running away from God, we ought to run to God and take responsibility for any wrongdoing (Psalm 50:15). Running from God or passing blame only prolongs the learning experience which is often painful and difficult. David, Paul and other faithful can be referred to as persons after God's heart. They cherished their relationship with God more than men. They took responsibility for their errors and ran to God, the opposite of what Adam, Cain and many others do.

Make a choice to start obeying God, even at the point of giving up your life to do the right thing and God will give life to everything dead around you. Abraham loved God more than his son Isaac, and God spared his son's life (Genesis 22:12–13). Queen Esther made a choice to risk her life and go before the king against royal protocol and the law, to plead for the very survival of the Jewish people in captivity in Persia, and

God honored her and granted her request (Esther 4:14–16). Shadrach, Meshach and Abednego loved God and were willing to die in the furnace. God himself showed up in the fire (Daniel 3:25), Daniel reverenced God even to the death, and God sent an angel to shut the mouths of the lions (Daniel 6:22).

Today we read about these great men and women because they used their power of choice to love God more than their own lives (John 12:25). We have the responsibility to make choices that are aligned to divine principles and like them, use our choices to impact our lives and those around us.

Chapter 28

Pathways to Success

The ultimate fulfillment in life is continuously dwelling in God's presence and doing what he originally intended for your life, as opposed to doing what seems good to you, your family, guardians, mentors, peers, instructors and idols. Succeeding in an assignment that is not God's original intent for your life might be good and even prove to be "successful," but it is failure in the eyes of God. Many parents coax or impose their unfulfilled goals unto their children, which robs the children of their God-ordained success.

The world today has many graduates with accolades, yet they have broken dreams, buried aspirations, and delusional definitions of success. Some successful billionaires commit suicide because of the void within. God, who put the seed of success in every one of us, insists that we abide in him to bear the right fruit (John 15:5). Seeds have the inherent ability to become "fruit trees." The fruit tree, which is the future of the seed, already exists in it. God, who created humans, put seed in them and commanded them to bear fruit—"Be fruitful and multiply" (Genesis 1:28). As seeds need the right ground to be fruitful, so do we need God's presence to bear righteous fruits and obtain right success.

Our purpose for existence was established before we were conceived in our mothers' wombs (John 1:13). Everyone has the responsibility to discover and walk in their pre-determined purpose. God, speaking through prophet Jeremiah said, "Before I formed you in the womb I knew you; before you were born I sanctified you [set apart]; I ordained [appointed] you a prophet to the nations" (Jeremiah 1:5). By implication we have a predestined aspect of life buried in our hearts called success.

Jesus echoed this in another way: "You did not choose Me, but I chose you and appointed you that you should go and bear fruit" (John 15:16). While writing to the believers in Ephesus, Paul, the Apostle to the Gentiles, said, "He chose us in Him before the foundation of the world, that we should be holy and without blame before Him in love" (Ephesians 1:4). Holiness, righteousness, and right success are coded in our DNA.

God desires that every one of his children has right success; that is, succeeding in what he created them to do. This is our divine assignment or work, not a job. A job is meant to provide the skills or funds needed to do the work. When we derail from our God-given assignment, work becomes toil. This happened to Adam and Eve when they disobeyed God. The work they had previously enjoyed, became toil when they were driven out of God's presence unto cursed ground (Genesis 2:15; 3:17).

We should always remember that our future is God's past (Psalm 139:16). God is committed to the future he placed in us, that is why he often shows the end at the beginning (Isaiah 46:9–10). Our responsibility is to align ourselves to God's purpose, plan and chart out the course to our destiny with him (Proverbs 19:21). We should not live in our past but learn from it. Even though Jesus by his death paid the price to salvage our future, we must dwell in his presence and surrender to the process of conception, germination, and growth to bring forth the right fruits.

The number one strategy of the enemy is to get us out of God's presence, so we bear bad fruits, "good" fruits that are not right, or none at all. In the temptation of Jesus, the devil quoted the right scripture for the wrong purpose. Quite often, the devil will tempt us to run ahead of God, which could lead to an abortion of destiny or premature death. Here are some examples of biblical figures who waited on God's timing; David was anointed king long before he ascended the throne, however, he continued to serve his father and brothers and gained experience from killing the lion and the bear. This experience prepared him to face and defeat Goliath (1 Samuel 16–17). Likewise, Jesus, who was worshiped as King at birth, only manifested at age thirty. In between he had to grow in wisdom and stature, gaining favor with God and man (Luke 2:52).

God's inspiration and timing of the purpose in us is always yielding. He allows us the season to grow, study in the background before any exposure, just like farmers do when they prepare seedlings, replant and prune them that they may bear more fruit (John 15:1).

This is also seen in other fields such as manufacturing, where manufacturers determine the purpose of their product and are keen to see the product succeed to protect the name and reputation of the company. God is the chief manufacturer who sets the end from the beginning, as succinctly captured by Jeremiah saying, "For I know the thoughts that I think toward you, says the Lord, thoughts of peace and not of evil, to give you a future and a hope" (Jeremiah 29:11). The potential to succeed is embedded in every human and the Creator is on the watch out to protect his name and achieve his objective for creating mankind. Hence, even when mankind rebelled against him, he still sent Jesus to salvage his eternal plan for creating the world and mankind.

Any man who repents and returns to the Lord is reintroduced to himself and given the keys to pursue right success. God never allows the believer to gamble with life or claim the popular saying, "God helps those who help themselves."[52] In the old dispensation, God inspired men like Joshua to read and meditate on the law day and night in order to have good success (Joshua 1:8). In that dispensation, they only had the law (Torah or Pentateuch) without the spirit of the law, whereas in the new dispensation, the road map to right success is captured in the entire constitution of God from Genesis to Revelation. In the new dispensation, believers have the entire Word of God and the Holy Spirit who reveals God's mind to convict and remind the believers of the truth (John 14:26; 1 Corinthians 2:11). In this regard, as believers we have everything at our disposal to discover what we were born to do, make plans, acquire the necessary skills, and continue to seek divine guidance to achieve right success.

Corruption and shortcuts exhibit man's lack of trust in God and their intention to succeed without him. God maintains that true success and promotion come neither from the east (occultism), west (education) nor south (connections) but from the north, the throne of God (Psalm 75:6–7). The journey to right success should start from the north, Mount Zion on the side of the North, and the city of the great King (Psalm 48:2). As we take our bearing from the north, the spirit of the King will order our footsteps. Success stories that take root or depend on occult powers, accolades and connections may seem good but with time the bitter truth takes effect. God wants his product, you, and me, to depend on him alone.

It should be noted that, success is not luck, it is predictable. It is purpose based and revolves around the identification of problems and the development of needed skills to solve them (Ecclesiastes 10:10), obedience to natural and spiritual principles of success (Matthew 16:19; Joshua 1:8) and the readiness to defy human "laws" (rules and traditions) that contradict divine principles.

There is no room for shortcuts or corruption to attain success in the kingdom. The rush for wealth without work causes many to choose shortcuts overdue process. Today's "microwave success" eliminates process, which results in a generation of perverts who seek miracles and not the valuable lessons gained through process. Individuals who indulge in corruption, manipulation, and deception to achieve success reflect their unbelief in God's ability to meet their needs and provide a way of escape in difficult circumstances.

When we believe in Jesus, we receive the Holy Spirit who realigns our desires to God's will and helps us focus on the source rather than the resources. This means God has our best interest than anyone or anything else.

The ability to be patient and wait on God for provision is the test of trust. Sarah and Abraham took this test and failed. Rather than wait on God to fulfil his word regarding the birth of the promised son, Isaac, they decided to take a shortcut that resulted in the conception, birth, and eventual banishment of Ishmael (Genesis 16). Jesus, however, rejected the shortcut satan offered him to get back the kingdoms of the world (Matthew 4:8–9). He wanted to earn the kingdoms back God's way (Luke 22:42). The litmus test of trust is the ability to do things God's way regardless of time, internal and external pressures of life. So, stealing to satisfy your need, corrupting your way out of situations, sex outside of marriage to meet desires, coaxing or hype messages for people to give to God are all shortcuts.

We are equipped to face challenges and overcome them. We overcome circumstances by considering and applying God's will and promises to situations rather than focusing and pondering on the challenges. When we focus on the problem, we give it authority over us, but when we focus on the Word of God regarding the situation the problem diminishes, while our trust in God magnifies. As a matter of fact, we are encouraging ourselves in the Lord as King David did in times of fear and distress (1 Samuel 30:6; 1 Corinthians 10:13).

Whenever, we receive a bad report, we have a choice on whose report to believe and focus on, in thoughts, words and deeds. All that the senses perceive are in the natural realms, but their roots are in the spiritual. That does not mean we ignore the bad report but change our focus, then make plans to solve the problem, based on the Master's word regarding the situation. Believers who are grounded are not moved by what they see, hear, feel, smell or touch because senses can be deceptive, and God did not call us to live by them but by faith. We are to focus on what is written concerning the situation as opposed to the problem (Hebrews 12:2).

The saying that only God can change the world is but a myth. It may sound good and very spiritual but not entirely true. God does not have the final say in anyone's life or events on earth. God restored man's legal authority over the earth through the death and resurrection of Jesus. Which implies that we have the final say in the affairs of our lives and the sovereign right to determine what happens be it right, good, or bad on the earth.

Yes, God is all powerful! But he cannot break his own word (Isaiah 55:11). He has power but handed over the switch to man. Like a powerhouse that supplies electricity to our homes, God placed the responsibility of turning on or off the lights in our lives in our hands. Despite the power God possesses, he cannot turn the switches in our lives on. He always needs a man to work with. For example, to destroy Sodom and Gomorrah consulted with Abraham, to deliver Israel from Egypt, he sent Moses and to restore man's dominion over the earth he gave his begotten son. Today his strategy forges on. He works with the believer to legally pull down all forms of wickedness and replace them with his kingdom's culture.

God will never task anyone with anything that he has not equipped them to do. This is why we have the Holy Spirit to guide and not compel or control us to do all that the Lord requires of us. On the contrary, the one who schemes, controls, compels and manipulates mankind into doing his bidding regardless, is the devil. Even after he was defeated by Jesus and all authority returned to man, the devil still attempts to blind mankind from accepting the truth. As it is written, "Our gospel is veiled to those who are perishing, whose minds the god of this age has blinded, who do not believe lest the light of the gospel of the glory of Christ, who is the image of God, should shine upon them" (2 Corinthians 4:3–4).

The challenges and struggles the enemy brings to believers are targeted to weaken and destroy their belief system (faith in God). Our belief system, on which our faith anchors, is what moves and pleases God. Jesus said, "If you can believe, all things are possible to him who believes" (Mark 9:23). And Paul, in his letter to the Hebrew believers, said, "But without faith it is impossible to please Him, for he who comes to God must believe that He is a rewarder of those who diligently seek Him" (Hebrews 11:6). Our belief system can be likened to a three-legged stool on which we comfortably rest our weight having the conviction that it will hold and support us.

The "stool of faith" or our belief system, gives us access to kingdom favor for effective living. Our faith, like a three-legged stool, is held up by three actions—TRUTH, TRUST and OBEDI-ENCE. These can otherwise be referred to as the three pillars of our belief system. The first leg is TRUTH, which is based on the true knowledge of God, even as Jesus said, "And you shall know the truth and the truth will make you free" (John 8:32). This truth is the original intent for creation and the foundational building block of trust in the will of the Creator. The second is TRUST, as it is written, "Trust in the Lord with all your heart..." (Proverbs 3:5). Your trust to confidently sit on a three-legged stool depends on your understanding that it will carry and secure your weight. In that light, in order to trust God, we should know the truth about him and his existence, as written in his Word (Psalm 9:10). The third action is OBEDIENCE, rooted in what Jesus said: "If you love Me keep My commandments" (John 14:15).

The principle pillar of our belief system is truth, which is the knowledge of who God is and his intention for creation. You can only trust someone you know. It is absurd to claim to know and trust God without obeying him. Scripture has it that the fear of the Lord is the beginning of wisdom, which means when you know the truth about God, you will trust him and obey his Word. True knowledge of God entails the truth about who he is, why he created you, the world, and the earth. Trusting him is accepting him as your Lord—your owner. God is king and his Word is law to all of creation, so your obedience must be complete and unquestionable because you know who he is and all that he stands for.

Truth, trust, and obedience to God do not go unnoticed. The devil has strategies or schemes to dislocate the pillars on which faith stands (1 Peter 5:8). To dislocate the pillar of truth he breeds ignorance, to break trust in God he sows seeds of fear and doubt, and finally, to impede obedience he promotes lawlessness. Satan is true to his name, the prince of darkness whose reign is characterized by ignorance, deception, and lawlessness. He is a trick star, a master manipulator who utilizes the weapons of deception, ignorance, fear, and disobedience to their fullest because he is aware of the looming destruction coming his way (Revelation 12:12). The kingdom book cites that, the only fight to be fought is the good fight of faith to counteract the devices of the enemy (1 Timothy 6:12). That is believing in the finished work of Jesus at the cross and walking in the victory made available to us (1 Corinthians 15:57).

The numerous challenges the devil throws at us to trigger fear and doubt are geared toward destroying our belief system. Adam and his wife, out of fear of their action against the Word of God, hid themselves from God's presence (Genesis 3:8–10). Because of fear, Job's hedge of defense against the attacks of the devil was broken, he confessed saying, "For the thing I greatly feared has come upon me" (Job 3:25). Fear continues to blind many from accepting the finished work of Jesus. Jesus dismantled the schemes of the devil, restored our dominion, and put us in-charge again to do what is right not just good. We are overcomers when we choose to know the truth, trust, and obey God. We have the responsibility to control our emotions, tame our tongues and stand our ground when the enemy attacks.

Our belief in God and obedience to his word are the mainstay of getting things done on the earth. The god of this age, whose wisdom is corrupt, blinds non-believers with material gains and believers with religious activities in an effort to manipulate and get them out of the presence of God. He capitalizes on our ignorance that God through Jesus made us more than conquerors. We have the tools to choose rightly to disallow the devil from decimating our lives and corrupting the governing systems on earth. Therefore, we are to guard our hearts with all diligence for from it flows the issues of life (Proverbs 4:23). We also have angels that have been assigned to heed our instructions and protect us from any harm (Psalm 34:7; 103:20).

The keys to right success are in our hands. As sons, who are led by the Spirit, we have the authority by the Word of God in the name of Jesus to pursue knowledge of the truth, and trust what God says about us that we may achieve right success through obedience to his Word. God has given us wisdom to use our gifting and has made our mouths like sharp swords (Isaiah 49:2; Luke 21:15) to declare our authority and take total control of the affairs of life on earth, while making the earth look like heaven.

Chapter 29

Kingdom Talk—Hearing the Voice of God

The choices we make in life shape our destinies. They are underpinned by the voices we hear from within and without. The competing voices come from both the natural and spiritual realms. From the spiritual realm there exists two voices: God's and the devil's. In the natural realm we have two voices as well: our own inner voice and that of the surroundings. You and I have the responsibility to distinguish between these voices.

To hear and discern the voice of God from other voices, we must know him first. Jesus told the religious leaders, "The sheep follow the shepherd because they know his voice, yet they will by no means follow a stranger, but will flee from him, for they do not know the voice of strangers" (John 10:4–5). He continued, "My sheep hear My voice, and I know them, and they follow Me" (v. 27).

We can only know God by the revelation of the truth in his Word. The challenge with many New Testament saints is the reluctance to study the Word, get to know God for themselves and pay the price of seeking knowledge and understanding in order to effectively apply the principles (Proverbs 4:7). Quite often, many modern day saints feed the ego of the so-called powerful men of God by asking, encouraging, adoring, and even paying these men to go and seek God on their behalf. This is identical to what the children of Israel did in the wilderness when they said to Moses, "You speak with us, and we will hear; but let not God speak with us, less we die" (Exodus 20:19).

God's desire has always been and still is to speak directly to everyone. In the new covenant, God speaks to all believers by his Spirit, the inner voice in them. God never addressed Jesus with an audible voice but spoke from within him. The audible voice at the baptism of Jesus and at the Mount of Transfiguration was not intended for him but the people (Matthew 3:17; 17:5). God shared his thoughts with Jesus and wants to do the same with all of us. He is more interested in thinking through us, than speaking to us.

The Holy Spirit, also called the Spirit of truth, is the voice of the Word of God inside of you. Jesus said, "The words that I speak to you are spirit, and they are life" (John 6:63). The saints in the Old Testament had the laws but not the spirit of the law. Hence, God had to speak to them through prophets, on whom the Holy Spirit came upon at specific moments to tell them what to say to the people. By reason of the fall, generations were born alien to their home country which resulted in

God having to speak to them by his audible voice, or through the prophets. God speaking through prophet Isaiah said, "Behold, the Lord's hand is not shortened, that he cannot save; nor His ear heavy, that it cannot hear, but your iniquities have separated you from your God; and your sins have hidden His face from you, so that He will not hear" (Isaiah 59:1–2).

Unfortunately, God had to speak to his people through prophets, who were middlemen or messengers. These methods of communication were flawed and subject to misinterpretation and interferences. Second-hand information is often subject to distortion, even as speaking through middlemen is cumbersome, as words are lost in translation, or even worse the messengers can be off script. Many messengers and middlemen have been proven to deceive and manipulate the receiver of the information.

In times past, God wanted to talk to his delivered children so dearly that he used all kinds of ways to talk to them, like the burning bush experience with Moses, the talking donkey with Balaam and the writings on the wall to king Belshazzar (Exodus 3:2; Numbers 22:28; Daniel 5:5, 25). One can now understand why God changed the communication channel and method in the New Testament. It is written, "This is my beloved Son. Hear Him!" (Luke 9:35). "God, who at various times and in various ways spoke in time past to the fathers by the prophets, has in these last days spoken to us by His Son, whom He has appointed heir of all things, through whom also He made the worlds" (Hebrews 1:1–2). Therefore, whatever Jesus said and continues to say is by the Word and Spirit. As one under authority, he speaks not of his own mind but that of his Father, and by the help of the Holy Spirit, he is able to teach, remind and convict us of all things (John 16:13; 14:26).

Having an indwelling helper and counselor is more glorious than hearing external voices because when there is poor connection, interference, or a shutdown of the entire network one is not left in a precarious situation. The Bible says we have a better covenant than the old, where God had to speak as a master would to his servants and not to his sons. Paul speaking to the New Testament saints said, "After those days says the Lord: 'I will put my laws in their mind and write them on their hearts; and I will be their God and they shall be my people. None of them shall teach his neighbor, and none his brother, saying, 'Know the Lord, for all shall know Me, from the least of them to the greatest of them" (Hebrews 8:8–11). In that regard, in this dispensation we are spoken to not as servants but sons (believers).

As sons, the Father speaks to us by his Spirit that dwells in us (John 14:16-17). No father would love to communicate secrets to his sons via servants or 'men of God'. Sons have an inheritance (Ephesians 1:3) and do not need anyone to affirm or pronounce blessings upon them. The Old Testament premise of God using prophets (Amos 3:7; Hosea 12:13) to deliver, preserve and address his people were foreshadows of Jesus who is now our only savior, deliverer, mediator and high priest (Hebrew 4:14; 12:24).

Every believer has the Holy Spirit on the inside and God leaves the responsibility of hearing him to them. Since the voice is from the inside and is aligned to the word they have heard, read, and meditated upon, they will know if the voice they hear is that of Daddy or not. No child can miss the voice of his or her parents, neither would any parent love to talk to their offspring through others. As students in the kingdom school of thought, studying the word and asking the teacher within to guide us in all truth, whilst listening carefully to hear the voice of the word inside us regardless of the mood, time and place is a lifeline to effective communication, and our utmost priority.

If God speaks to us according to his word and by the gentle voice of the Holy Spirit then one may ask, what is the role of the prophets in the fivefold ministry commissioned by Jesus? They are to give direction to the body of Christ. Whatever they speak must be in right alignment with the written word. Many at times, God has to speak to the saints via the prophets because they are not listening to the voice of the Holy Spirit within, neither do they know his word. And even when he speaks through the prophets we are called to examine the prophecy against the Word of God, for it is written, "Beloved, do not believe every spirit, but test the spirits, whether they are of God; because many false prophets have gone out into the world" (1 John 4:1). Testing the spirit should not be viewed negatively because it enables the believer to probe and prove the source of the message in the prophecy (1John 4:1).

When God speaks from the outside by an audible voice or by a prophet, it is an event, just as Elijah stood and declared a three-year drought in the presence of the Lord (1 Kings 17:1) and later at mount Carmel, called fire from heaven to consume the sacrifice (1 Kings 18:37–38). Despite these great events, when he was threatened by Jezebel, the wife of king Ahab, he ran for his life and even prayed that he may die (1 Kings 19:1–14). Why? Because these wonders were events by the Spirit of God from the outside, that came and passed. But when the Holy Spirit dwells within you the miraculous becomes a lifestyle and the consciousness that he who is in you is greater than he who is in the world emboldens and empowers you not to run but stand before any form of opposition (1 John 4:4).

Humans are vessels that carry three types of thought: right, good, or bad thoughts. Our thoughts could be right, good, or even bad depending on the influence of our upbringing, learning experience, associations, traditions, and cultural backgrounds. On the other hand, the Creator's thoughts are aligned to his righteousness. Thoughts that are contrary to God's Word embody the nature of the devil as a liar and the source of all deception (John 8:44). We are admonished not to be conformed to the patterns of this world but to be transformed by the renewing of our minds. In so doing, we will be able to test and approve what God's good, acceptable, and perfect will is for us (Romans 12:2). Therefore, we should guard our hearts with all diligence for out of them spring the issues of life (Proverbs 4:23)

God's thoughts are written in scripture, they are peaceful and are revealed to us by his Spirit. Our minds are transformed when we listen, read, study, and meditate on his word. Having God's thoughts in our minds and hearts act as filters to our thoughts and the deceptions of the devil. In any given situation the Holy Spirit will remind us of the Word of God hidden in our hearts that we may choose between the truth of God and the lie of the devil. The question now is whose voice are you meditating and acting upon and whose words have you hidden in your heart (Psalm 119:11)?

Natural law dictates that one exudes what is loaded on the inside. If you load junk inside your heart, you will sound like it, look like it and even behave like it. As the saying goes, "garbage in garbage out." This was the implication of what Jesus explained to the Pharisees when they asked him why his disciples were transgressing the traditions of the elders by not washing their hands when they ate bread. He said, "Not what goes into the mouth defiles a man: but what comes out of the mouth, this defiles the man…, whatever enters the mouth goes into the stomach and is eliminated? But those things which proceed out of the mouth come from the heart, and they defile a man. For out of the heart proceed evil thoughts, murder, adulteries, fornications, thefts, false witness, blasphemies" (Matthew 15:11–19). Therefore, you need to hear, study, discern and meditate into your spirit the right Word of God.

In Paul's writing to the Philippian Church he said, "Whatever things are true, whatever things are noble, whatever things are just, whatever things are pure, whatever things are lovely, whatever things are of good report, if there is any virtue and if there is anything praise worthy meditate on these things" (Philippians 4:8). So you can behave and look like God.

All of creation is eagerly expecting to hear and obey the voice of the sons of God, who have been redeemed by the blood of the Lamb of God and are led by his Spirit. Let us not forget that the Holy Spirit is a helper not a compulsive or a controlling spirit. He will not remind you of things you have not taken time to deposit in your spirit. This can be likened to attempting to withdraw money from an account at an automated machine you know you did not make deposits into.

We have the responsibility to deposit the Word of God in our subconsciousness or heart, because if we do not, the Holy Spirit will have nothing to remind us of. Or if we have God's Word in our heart but decide to ignore the counsel of the Holy Spirit, he remains silent and consequently we continue to fall prey to the external voices. The Holy Spirit only works at our request and never controls us. In that regard, listening to him in this dispensation is paramount to distinguishing between the voice of God and other voices. His presence in us allows God to think through us as he did with Adam before he fell and Jesus when he walked the earth.

Chapter 30

Kingdom Court Room of Prayer

Petitioning the king is a fundamental principle in kingdom living. We pray because we want to give God the legal right to intervene in the realm of our sovereign authority. Satan, the devil, is our number one adversary who relentlessly challenges our God-given authority on the earth. Jesus who overcame him and restored our authority is our advocate or mediator when we pray (Hebrews 9:15). The Holy Spirit, who is our Counselor, reminds us of what to say to counter the devil's accusations.

Prayer is a legal setting that is solemn, sacred, and based on law not on emotions, feelings, or hearsay. Quite often, it takes on the form of a courtroom with Jesus as our mediator and advocate, arguing our case before God, the righteous judge, who refers to the constitution and grants our rights. Considering this, we cannot lose a court proceeding except, we are held in contempt, ignorant of our rights or worse as children of the Judge, be found to have broken the law. When in the kingdom courtroom of prayer and supplication, we are to pray and make known our requests based on legal rights accorded to us in the constitution— the Word of God.

You will recall that the natural reflects the spiritual (2 Corinthians 4:18). Our courtrooms and their proceedings reflect how we should approach prayer in the kingdom. We should acknowledge the positions and roles of the parties involved, that is; God as judge, Jesus as advocate, the Holy Spirit as counselor, the devil as accuser, while you and I as defendants on trial.

In the courtroom of prayer, even though the judge is our father and Jesus our elder brother our advocate, we are required to state our case in line with the constitution because the courtroom represents the country, not family business. As the popular saying goes, justice is blind, meaning it is impartial and objective regardless of status, creed, race, or gender. As law-abiding citizens of the kingdom of heaven, we need to understand and apply the following:

- Know and understand that God is a righteous judge (right-giver) and makes judgment based on the constitution, not on emotions, charisma, and hearsay doctrines.
- Jesus is the Advocate (mediator), defending our rights as promised in the constitution.
- The Holy Spirit is our Counselor and brings to our remembrance what the constitution says about us and what the mediator has done for us to obtain favor before the judge.

- As the defendants on trial, we have the responsibility to know, understand and apply the constitution rightly with the guidance of the counselor.
- The devil, who is the accuser of the brethren, will often cite the constitution out of context to lead us to ignore our legal counsel, misquote and contradict the constitution in order to make us inevitably lose our case before the righteous judge.

Kingdom citizenship and right alignment with the constitution is the key to obtaining favor with the righteous judge, who is the King of the universe. The King does all things for good and for his good pleasure (Romans 8:28; Philippians 2:13), according to his original intention. So, whenever you address the King, you say "Your Majesty" first and then make your petition according to what is on his heart, which is the prosperity of his citizens and the advancement of his kingdom (Matthew 6:9-10). Once you do this, you immediately secure the king's favor.

In the patterns of answered prayers below, we see God's interest as priority.

- Israel cried out to God and was delivered from Egypt for God's purpose and pleasure—to serve him (Exodus 3:12; 4:23).
- Hannah prayed for a son and got an immediate answer once she placed God's interest first (1 Samuel 1:11).

- ➤ David defeated Goliath on the platform of kingdom interest—to stop the Philistines from defying the armies of the living God (1 Samuel 17:26).
- ➤ The return of the Holy Spirit is to make the believer a witness of Jesus and a representative of God's government on earth (Acts 1:8).
- ➤ Joseph's dream and Samson's power were all to serve God's purpose—to save and preserve God's people in times of famine, conflict, and war (Genesis 45:5; Judges 13:5)
- ➤ God gives us the power to get wealth for his covenant's sake, so that we can impact the world with his culture (Deuteronomy 8:18).

In the courtroom of prayer, kingdom priorities are non-negotiable. Our citizenship and right alignment to the constitution gives us the authority to demand our rights and privileges. The kingdom constitution reiterates this by saying, "Seek first the kingdom of God and his righteousness, and all these things shall be added to you" (Matthew 6:33). James, the apostle, articulated very well the reason why believers miss the mark when they pray, by saying, "You ask and do not receive, because you ask amiss, that you may spend it on your pleasures" (James 4:3). Rather than seek God's ways and priorities most of us seek his acts. God's signs and wonders are meant to follow the believer not the reverse.

In the old covenant, signs and wonders were used by God to cause the children of Israel to know and follow him. However, in the new covenant, our citizenship and calling are based on the finished work of Jesus at the cross. The cross was the platform on which we transited from "bless me Lord" pattern of prayer to "let thy will be done on earth as it is in heaven." Though signs and wonders are important, they are events that come and go. By implication, our prayer agenda should be aimed at making the world function like heaven, which is a transformational process not just an event. This may appear impossible with man but with God all things are possible. This possibility was made through the "great exchange" that took place at the cross, as Jesus cried out, "It is finished!"

As our advocate in the courtroom of prayer, Jesus argues our case based on his finished work and the great exchange. On the grounds of the latter, a "Trust Fund" was established in heavenly places (Ephesians 1:3). We were redeemed and have been given the power of attorney to sign into the trust account, using the name of Jesus. The great exchange described in Isaiah 53, revealed the components of the established trust fund:

- Jesus became sin that we may become God's righteousness.
- His body was wounded so that by his stripes we are healed.
- He was rejected and became a man of sorrow so that we prosper in all things.

The Holy Spirit is the administrator of this trust fund established more than two thousand years ago. He is in us a counselor of our eternal blessings while Jesus is the mediator between the Father and us. With such wise council how can we lose! The Holy Spirit enables us to approach prayer with confidence, even as it is written, "Now this is the confidence that we have in Him, that if we ask according to His will, He hears us (1 John 5:14).

Therefore:

> Prayer should start with the knowledge of God's will on the situation. That is, knowledge of the keys or laws of the kingdom of heaven regarding the situation. God is a (i.e between our case and based) righteous judge, who upholds and protects the constitution (Psalm 7:11). He judges only by the law and has given us the spirit of the law and the righteousness of his Son.

> We are to put God in remembrance (Isaiah 43:26) of what he says in his Word regarding all situations because as sovereign beings we have a choice and God cannot impose his will on us.

> Believe that he has heard our prayers that are made according to his will, which he cannot deny, given that God has exalted his word above himself (Psalm 138:2).

> Walk in the consciousness of the answered prayers, while declaring his will until the desired change is manifested.

The results of prayer, like any legal proceeding, may take a while to manifest. The wait for a verdict is often long and sometimes tests our patience and the ability to hang on to God's promises. However, thanksgiving and right declarations keep us away from worrying, complaining, murmuring, fearing, and doubting. During the period of waiting, we should watch out for the enemy because he may show us contrary situations to cause us to lose faith in God and consequently solicit advice from disbarred advocates and kangaroo courts. These attempts to obtain justice, freedom and find rest outside the constitutional provisions of the righteous judge end in futility.

Our belief in the finished work of Jesus, reinforces our trust in God's Word. Disobedience depletes our trust account into a negative balance (red), and when we repent, our balance returns to zero balance (amber). Thereafter we must rebuild our knowledge of the Word and obey to achieve a positive balance (green). Jesus paid the price for our transgressions and God forgives us, but we must be transformed in our minds to rebuild the trust account.

The prodigal son returned, and his father repositioned him into his sonship inheritance. However, one can only imagine the time and effort it must have taken to rebuild his image and regain the trust of his family. Returning to God and believing in his salvation agenda re-introduces you to what you lost but that does not negate the process of changing your thought patterns and realigning your values and choices to those of the kingdom.

The name of Jesus is cardinal in our new covenant walk with God. His name reminds the father of his obedience to all the laws and sacrifice at the cross. Under the old covenant one had to faithfully keep all the commandments to receive all the blessings in Deuteronomy 28. Once one was broken, all were virtually broken and the blessings lost (James 2:10). For instance:

> ➤ Moses broke one law by striking the rock with the rod instead of speaking to it as God had commanded him and never entered the promised land (Numbers 20:7–12),
> ➤ Achan broke one law by stealing from the spoils of war and caused Israel to be defeated in the battle at Ai; and he, his family and belongings were destroyed as a result (Joshua 7:18–26).

Jesus kept all the laws, including circumcision, dedication, attended all the Old Testament festivals and even accepted to be baptized by John (Matthew 3:13–17; 5:17). He fulfilled all the laws on our behalf and laid down his life and paid the price for our sin. He is now the compassionate high priest interceding on our behalf to plead our case before the father even when we stumble. His earthly journey in human form enabled him to understand our weaknesses and with this, he encourages us to approach the throne of grace with boldness, so that we may obtain mercy and find grace to help us in time of need (Hebrews 4:14–16).

The key to having judgment in our favor from the courtroom of prayer is having an understanding of our constitutional rights and acknowledging the various roles played by the parties in the courtroom, that is, the judge, advocate, counselor and the accuser. They all stand on these principles to exercise their roles: The judge on the constitution to deliver righteous verdicts, the advocate on the great exchange to assure the accused of the price paid, the Holy Spirit, the Counselor on the Word of God in you, to remind you of your rights and the accuser on your ignorance to rob you of the great exchange entitlement.

Above all, as believers, we should seek to know and understand the purpose of prayer, the right approach to the "kingdom courtroom of prayer," the intent of the Advocate and Counselor in securing our freedom and restoring our authority to dominate the world.

Chapter 31

Kingdom Prosperity

The source of all resources is the Creator. He is a king and his honor is seen in the prosperity of his citizens. All the resources placed by God above, on and under the earth and in the waters are intended for his royal family to use and make the earth function like heaven. In that regard, prosperity in the kingdom is having all our needs met by the source for the purpose of rebuilding his kingdom on earth.

The prerogative for prosperity in the kingdom is good stewardship and effective management of all resources placed at our disposal by God to dominate the earth. Emphasis should then be placed on understanding and accepting the great exchange package, which includes freedom from sin, health, and the restored relationship with our father in heaven, rather than just material and financial wealth.

The restored dominion mandate over the earth that is given to the sons of God is all about stewardship and not ownership.

Adam and Eve, for example, were tasked with the management, cultivation, and expansion of the garden and all that was within it throughout the earth. God never gave them the deed of ownership of the earth and all its fullness but a management contract. This contract of all global resources was not meant to create poverty, breed oppression and dominion of other humans but was intended to bring the culture of the kingdom of heaven to the earth. However, after the fall, the systems were corrupted, and mankind lost their citizenship right to steward God's resources rightfully.

More than 2000 years ago Jesus gave the keys of kingdom prosperity to the church to 'dig up' wealth and bless generations (Matthew 16:19). In all nations of the world, citizens who are ignorant of the rights and privileges promised in the constitution will not know or understand how to claim them. Many kingdom citizens—believers, are no different. They die with riches 'under their feet'. God never gave Adam and Eve a chair or a car, 'he put the chair in the tree and the car in the ground'. He blessed them and instructed them to be fruitful and multiply (Genesis 1:28).

Ignorance on how to use the keys of the kingdom has kept believers frustrated, broke and praying to escape the world. Access to kingdom prosperity depends on your knowledge, understanding and use of the keys in your area of gifting (Hosea 4:6). No amount of prosperity gospel declarations, worship and praise, sowing of 'seeds' or even your 'love' for God alone can make you subdue the earth and be wealthy. Prayer, fasting, seed sowing are not wrong but should be used in their rightful context.

Good stewardship of resources attracts God's blessings. There is no record of our first parents prior to the fall, fasting, praying or even sowing seed to be prosperous. They were created and given wealth and all that God required of them was good and purposeful stewardship. This pattern of prosperity is what Jesus restored to all.

The Old Testament pattern of prosperity was based on works of the law and giving to receive. One had to obey all the commandments of God to receive the blessings, or they were cursed as outlined in Deuteronomy 28. The New Testament contract returns us to the relationship man had with God in the Eden garden before the fall. This re-birth or reconnection to our source restores our citizenship rights and privileges. In addition, God has given us the power of attorney in the name of Jesus to cash into the trust fund that was established when Jesus said, "It is finished!" and died. By his death, he took away our iniquities, sorrows, and poverty, and gave us divine prosperity. Yet, many live their lives ignorant of their "salvation ticket on the cruise ship of life." As redeemed sons sailing with the Father, Son and Spirit on the cruise ship of life all our needs are covered. Instead of carrying supplies to the cruise ship, we should believe that the ticket bought on our behalf covers 100 percent of all our needs.

In the kingdom the king is obliged to provide for his citizens and make them prosperous. The challenge arises when the citizens fail to understand and apply the concept of lordship to their daily lives. They confess Jesus as their Lord and Master but remain in-charge; secondly many citizens lack management skills, and never make plans to present to God so that he can order their footsteps. As it is written, "Many are the plans in a man's heart, but it is the Lords purpose that will prevail" (Proverbs 19:21). It is therefore our responsibility to make Jesus the Lord of our lives, and ensure our plans line up with God's purpose and then make known our request for resources to execute the plans (Habakkuk 2:2).

The wise and rich king, Solomon, wrote this by the Spirit of God, saying, "The rich and the poor have this in common, the Lord is the maker of both of them all" (Proverbs 22:2). They were both created in God's image and likeness and born only with saliva in their mouths, none with a "silver spoon." God blessed and put seeds in them, then instructed them to be fruitful and multiply. Those who think, plan, invest and manage resources eventually become rich. On the other hand, those who do not put on their thinking cap, fold their hands, and go to sleep end up in poverty (Proverbs 24:33–34).

God does not tolerate poor planning and bad management. If you are a good steward he gives you more to manage, but if you are a poor manager of your resources and those of others, God withdraws his financial flow from your life and even makes sure the little you have is taken away and given to others who can manage (Matthew 25:14–30).

God weighs the intention of your request for resources than the request itself. Case in point, the reason why Nehemiah requested and received resources from king Artaxerxes, the king of Persia, was to rebuild the destroyed walls of the city of Jerusalem and not to fund his pleasures (Nehemiah 2). God does everything for his good pleasure, so he wants to know what the kingdom's interest in the request is. Even as it is written, "You ask and do not receive, because you ask amiss, that you may spend it on your pleasures" (James 4:3).

Hannah, mother of the prophet Samuel, prayed for several years for a child and heaven remained closed. The day she changed her prayer strategy and focused on God's interest, she conceived and bore a male child. Hannah made a vow: "O Lord of hosts, if You will indeed look on the affliction of Your maidservant and remember me and not forget Your maidservant, but will give Your maidservant a male child, then I will give him to the Lord all the days of his life.' ...So it came to pass in the process of time that Hannah conceived and bore a son, and called his name Samuel, saying, 'Because I have asked for him from the Lord;" (1 Samuel 1:11, 20). She was specific and knew exactly why she was making her request known to God. Therefore, we are to take honest inventories of our prayer lists and verify if indeed they prioritize the advancement of God's kingdom.

In the parable of the talents, Jesus concluded, "For to everyone who has, more will be given, and he will have abundance; but from him who does not have, even what he has will be taken away" (Matthew 25:29). God gives everyone according to their ability to steward his resources. Contrary to public expectations, God does not dish out money when we pray, he inspires us through ideas on what course to take to get what we are searching for to advance his kingdom. In that regard, when we pray for blessings, God gives us divine ideas to solve problems. Believers should then find problems, develop working plans, present them to the king and bring divine solutions to address them.

Solomon the wise king wrote, "A good man leaves an inheritance to his children's children. But the wealth of the sinner is stored up for the righteous" (Proverbs 13:22). Before you agree with this statement, stop, and think how the sinners got the riches in the first place. What are they doing differently from you? I submit this for your consideration, they plan, innovate, and effectively manage all resources in their care. Unbelievers understand problem-solving as the ladder to great riches. They may be sinners but understand and apply principles of stewardship thereby effectively managing all resources. Believers in this new dispensation, need to know, understand, and apply the principles of good stewardship to be successful and leave an inheritance to the next generation.

It was prophesied by Prophet Isaiah that Jesus would be despised and rejected; a man of sorrow, without esteem and acquainted with grief (Isaiah 53:3–4). Paul said, "For you know the grace of our Lord Jesus Christ that though He was rich, yet for your sakes He became poor, that you through His poverty might become rich" (2 Corinthians 8:9). It goes without saying that a poor citizen is an insult to the King and a disgrace in the kingdom. Christ exchanged his riches for our poverty more than two thousand years ago, so we as citizens of the kingdom of heaven could reflect the wealth of the government he died to restore.

Prosperity is part of our redemptive package, as it is written, "Blessed be the God and Father of our Lord Jesus Christ, who has blessed us with every spiritual blessing in the heavenly places in Christ" (Ephesians 1:3). Our belief in the redemptive work at the cross gives us access to the heavenly "Trust Fund" through the name of Jesus Christ. Once we draw from the account, we rejoice and thank God for the grace of divine provision. Like father Abraham who tithed to Melchizedek after the Most High had delivered and blessed him, we are to give tithes and offerings as thanksgivings for God's faithfulness (Genesis 14:20). Abraham never gave tithe by the law of works for the windows of heaven to be opened and pour blessings on him, rather he gave from the abundance he had received.

Tithes for prosperity were later introduced under the law of Moses and the prophets as a welfare system to support the Levite, the stranger, the fatherless and the widow in Israel (Deuteronomy 26:12–13). The tithes and offering of all their produce were kept in storehouses from where they were distributed. When the law of tithes and offerings were obeyed, the devourer was rebuked, and the windows of heaven opened, and blessings poured upon the people and all nations called Israel blessed. But when they disobeyed the laws, they were cursed for robbing God, as referenced in Malachi 3:8–12.

After Jesus fulfilled all the laws and became a curse for us, we were returned into the Eden dispensation of 24/7 open heaven and all spiritual wealth were made available to us to carry on the same assignment God had given to Adam. Paying tithes and offering sacrifices as was the case in the law and prophets was replaced by grace, for Jesus said he was the end of the law (Romans 10:4). Jesus admonished his ambassadors to use the spirit of the Old Testament welfare system of tithing to do the weightier or important matters of the law: justice, mercy, and faith (Matthew 23:23). Kingdom welfare giving is not based on the law but on grace, in order that everyone would have their needs met for the kingdom of heaven to advance (Acts 4:33–35).

Several prosperity gospel preachers have become like the scribes and Pharisees that Jesus rebuked in the gospel of Matthew saying, "Woe to you, scribes and Pharisees! For you tithe of mint and anise and cummin, and have neglected the weightier matters of the law: justice and mercy and faith. These you ought to have done, without leaving the others undone (Matthew 23:23). The preachers use the grace of Jesus to attract followers into their congregations but revert to the law where they pick and choose from the Word of God what serves their interest to extract and rob the followers.

Sowing of seeds and sacrifices with the sole purpose of receiving a recompense from God, after Jesus said, "It is finished!" is biblical misunderstanding or "spiritual corruption." Jesus restored our relationship with our heavenly father and our confidence as sons to approach him boldly. When Peter and Master Jesus had come to Capernaum, those who received the temple tax came to Peter and said, "Does your teacher not pay the temple tax?" He said, "Yes." And when he had come into the house Jesus anticipated him, saying, "What do you think Simon? From whom do the kings of the earth take customs or taxes, from their sons or from strangers?" Peter said to him, from strangers. Jesus said to him, "Then the sons are free" (Matthew 17:24–26). As sons according to the covenant transaction at Calvary, we were elevated from servants to shareholders in Daddy's "company." We have been realigned and repositioned to undertake our original assignment. Hence giving in this dispensation is out of gratitude and the restored relationship with our father in heaven.

Giving is a lifestyle in this dispensation. We should understand that we can never out give a king. Charles Spurgeon puts it this way, "It is beyond the realm of possibilities that one can have the ability to out give God."[53] We should be vigilant against the manipulations of the so called "men of God" who use all sorts of tactics, gimmicks, emotional frenzies and prophecies to extract resources from people, all in the name of giving to the king. This scheme of the prosperity gospel was never preached by Jesus, he preached the kingdom of heaven. Prosperity was just a result of the kingdom message he taught.

Reverend Benny Hinn, the great televangelist, acknowledged the deception of the prosperity gospel. He confessed that he too caught the cold when the devil sneezed and many other men of God continue to catch the prosperity gospel flu. In his own words he said, "The prosperity message has gone crazy, and am correcting my own theology; it's an offence to the Lord and hurtful to place a price on the gospel; the Holy Ghost is fed up with and grieved by it. Giving has become such a gimmick. I don't want to get to heaven and be rebuked. It is time we say it as it is, the gospel, blessings, miracles of God and prosperity are not for sale."[54] Other voices that have denounced the imbalanced nature of the prosperity gospel include that of the famous Televangelist Joyce Meyer. She admits that even her own prosperity gospel and faith went out of balance.[55]

The body of Christ, which is the church is not made of members but citizens of the kingdom of heaven and ambassadors on earth. Kingdom ambassadors should be as prosperous as the home country they represent. Their source of wealth should be rooted in the kingdom's commonwealth budget. Commonwealth is a kingdom principle, whereby the citizenry in a kingdom reflect their king's qualities, including his wealth and mindset. The king's reputation is tied to his people's welfare, unlike in a democracy where everyone is for themselves, for better or for worse and survival is for the fittest. This ideology is contrary to the values of the kingdom. The king's reputation is stained when any of his citizens is poor. This results in the world viewing him as irresponsible, limited in resources and unable to redeem his promises. Jesus illustrated this in his famous teaching, wherein he said that our heavenly father knows all that we need (Matthew 6:25–33).

All who have accepted the call into ministry should not beg or manipulate other citizens to sponsor their heavenly assignment. All their activities should be funded by the home country they represent. Their terms of reference (ToR), defined by the Lord of the harvest include a funding mechanism (Luke 10:2). When Jesus sent out the twelve apostles, he made their ToR very clear saying, "And as you go, preach, saying, The kingdom of heaven is at hand. Heal the sick, cleanse the lepers, raise the dead, cast out demons. Freely you have received, freely give. Provide neither gold nor silver nor copper in your money belts, nor bags for your journey, nor two tunics, nor sandals, nor staffs; for a laborer is worthy of his wages" (Matthew 10:7–10; 1 Timothy 5:18). It does not mean you do not need these things, but the supply is from above. The Lord may use any method, anyone, or anything to supply your needs. Trust him!

Jesus is Lord overall that includes over our lives, if we allow him. Once we make him Lord of our lives, he owns everything, and we have nothing. We should remember that, though we own nothing, we have all things by virtue of a father-son relationship (Luke 15:31). Adam and Eve before the fall, owned nothing but had everything. There is no record of them making sacrifices or bringing offerings to God to appease him to give them whatsoever they needed. These activities were consequences of the fall and Jesus restored us into the Eden dispensation. In this dispensation, we offer thanksgiving to the father for sending Jesus to die in our place, to Jesus for taking upon himself our sin, disease and poverty, and to the Holy Spirit for being our Helper, Comforter and Counselor.

Our stewardship obligation is to focus on the source for guidance to manage all his resources and fulfill his will. This implies diligence with resources, including time and talent. We should continuously seek wisdom from above to manage all resources placed in our care. God becomes furious with people who instead of managing resources turn around to worship them. He calls that idolatry, an insult to who he created us to be. How can mankind whom he created in his own image and conferred upon them his glory, turn around and share it with idols, to the extent of worshiping and calling money, animals, carved pieces of wood, stones and even themselves gods. Fellow ambassadors, there is work to be done and problems to be solved, so seeking counsel from other gods rather than the Creator of the universe makes our mission on earth impossible.

The world is searching for solutions to its problems. To be effective in providing them, we are expected to value the source over the resources. Recall, every problem is a business and our problem-solving skills make us prosperous. Like Moses solved the problem of slavery; David solved that of Goliath; Daniel solved the administrative problems of Babylon; Jesus solved the problem of sin and death and God exalted him. Considering this, we are not to pray quickly for problems to be removed, because they have the potential to introduce us to ourselves and add value. God does not necessarily protect us from all problems but uses them as avenues to reveal his kingdom's ability to provide and bless us through them. Testing reveals strength, just like a four-wheel vehicle attracts more value when it withstands tough and rough terrain.

The emerging global markets, one world economy and the rapid expansion of information, communication and technology will eventually pose serious challenges to the labor market and financial systems as we go deeper into the cashless society. One wonders if the church understands the implications posed by the emerging one world economy and high-tech communication systems. Do they have divine solutions to these challenges as Joseph and Daniel did, while in Egypt and Babylon respectively? (Genesis 41:37-44; Daniel 2:47-48) Is the church equipped to shine even as gross darkness envelops the world systems? If the answer is yes, then the church has the potential to cause many to rush into the kingdom for citizenship and be empowered to endure whatever menace the global economy throws at them.

If the answer is no, then the church needs to rise up, teach the right message that unveils and addresses the spiritual dimension and purpose of the global challenges. Let us not forget that there is a hidden agenda behind the emerging global systems, especially artificial intelligence, and the one-world government. These systems will be used by the anti-Christ to monitor and control the world. Scripture narrates scenes of church persecution, tribulations, the rapture and appearance of the anti-Christ.[56] These scenes are scary and might read as a script from a horror movie or some wild tale, but the Scriptures are usually on target and offer hope that the Lord Jesus will overcome the anti-Christ, destroy his one-world government, and then establish the heavenly kingdom government on earth with righteousness, justice, peace and joy.[57]

The anti-Christ, also referred to as the beast, is a man and his number is 666 (Revelation 13:16–18). He will emerge and cause those who will not want to take his name or his number on their right hand or on their foreheads, to not buy and sell, nor participate in the new world economy. Those who receive his mark will gain access to the global network frequency. By this frequency, they will be connected to the one-world government headed by him.[58] On the other hand, those who confess Jesus as Lord, bear the mark of Christ and are sealed by the Holy Spirit of promise. This Spirit connects believers to the heavenly government, which prohibits them from receiving the mark of the anti-Christ.[59]

The stage for such a dramatic phenomenon is unravelling before our eyes. The world is experiencing birth pangs of a new world order that would herald the one-world government. Such events include:

➤ The current global coronavirus pandemic and the politics surrounding the development of a vaccine[60];

➤ The Davos 2020 World Economic Forum on The Great Reset for the New World Order[61];

➤ Global financial crisis and conflicts;

➤ The Francesco Economy and its Global Pact to create a New Humanism[62].

All these are the perfect settings for the emergence of the anti-Christ who will promise to solve the global economic problems and bring lasting peace.

Besides the conflicts, health crisis, financial meltdown, and breach in security systems, there have been writings on the wall regarding events that would prelude the emergence of the anti-Christ. Many world powers have emerged, and more are yet to emerge. Currently we have the unions of the Europeans, Americans, Communists, Africans, Asians, and Arabs. From one of these entities the anti-Christ will rise. Biblical scholars point to the European Union as the most probable candidate, time can only tell.

The anti-Christ is expected to ride on the wings of the emerging one-world government, promising lasting peace, which many nations, including the United Nations, will buy into. The one-world government will mimic the tower of Babel (Genesis 11:4), but will be destroyed by a stone, cut without hands, typical to King Nebuchadnezzar's dream. The stone will crush it and establish the government of heaven on earth. Daniel recorded the king's dream saying, "You watched while a stone was cut without hands which stroke the image on its feet of iron and clay and broke them in pieces. ... And the stone that stroke the image became a great mountain and filled the whole earth" (Daniel 2:34–35; 6:26). The kingdom of King Jesus, the chief cornerstone, will eventually rubbish the one-world government and fill the whole earth with the heavenly governing system.

One may ask, why are these events important and how are they related to kingdom prosperity? Good question! These events send messages to prosperity gospel preachers, believers, and non-believers alike to be aware and prepare to face the looming global anarchy and socioeconomic upheavals. Messages that are not focused on the lordship of Jesus, his return, and his ability to protect and care for the kingdom's citizens will fall apart (Matthew 7:24–27).

There are references in the kingdom book that point to such times when desperate measures will require desperate actions. Many narratives in the Word of truth offer us hope and multiple scenarios with commonwealth principles for us to learn and prepare against future events. What a relief! Some of them include:

Prophet Elijah and the widow of Zarephath in 1 Kings 17: Elijah made a pronouncement of drought in the land, and when it happened God took care of him. God directed him to run to a brook and drink from it and then commanded ravens to bring him bread and meat in the morning and evening. And when the brook dried up, God told him to go and dwell in the house of a widow in Zarephath as he had commanded her to provide for him. With only a handful of flour and a little oil in a jar God preserved and fed Elijah, the widow, and her son till he sent rain on the earth.

Simon Peter and the full-fish-breaking net miracle in Luke 5:1–11: Simon Peter and three other fishermen had toiled all night and caught no fish. But Jesus said to Simon, "Launch out into the deep and let down your nets for a catch." It is recorded that Peter answered and said to him, "Master, we have toiled all night and caught nothing; nevertheless at your word I will let down the net." And when they had done this, they caught a great number of fish, and their net was breaking.

The miracle of the five loaves and two fish in Matthew 14:13–21: Jesus fed a great multitude that had followed him into a deserted place. He had compassion on them and healed the sick that were among them. The disciples justifiably requested to send the multitudes away to their homes from the deserted place as it had gotten late, to go find food. Jesus objected and told the disciples to feed them. The disciples said to him, "We have here only five loaves and two fish." He said to them, "Bring them here to Me." "Then he commanded the multitudes to sit down on the grass. And he took the five loaves and two fish, and looking up to heaven, he blessed and broke and gave the loaves to the disciples; and the disciples gave to the multitudes. So, they all ate and were filled, and they took twelve baskets full of the fragments that remained. Now those that had eaten were about five thousand men, besides women and the children."

Divine preservation, healing and supply of needs was the case when God protected and delivered Israel from Egypt (Psalm 105:15, 37): He visited Egypt with plagues and made a difference between his people the Israelites and the Egyptians, saying, "I will set apart the land of Goshen, in which My people dwell, that no flies shall be there...I will make a difference between the livestock of Israel and the livestock of Egypt. So that nothing shall die of all that belongs to the children of Israel" (Exodus 8:22; 9:4). It is also narrated how God brought Israel out of Egypt with a mighty hand and went before them. There was none feeble among them, he fed them with manna and quails (Exodus 16), brought water out of rocks (Exodus 17), went before them by day in pillar of cloud and by night in a pillar of fire to give them light (Exodus 13:21).

Money from least expected sources in Matthew 17:24–27: In this narrative Jesus points to the fact that strangers work for sons of the kingdom and God can provide from any source. At Capernaum, those who received the temple tax came to Peter and said, "Does your teacher not pay the temple tax?" He said, "Yes." And when he had come into the house Jesus anticipated him, saying, "What do you think Simon? From whom do the kings of the earth take customs or taxes, from their sons or from strangers?" Peter said to him, "From strangers." Jesus said to him, "Then the sons are free. Nevertheless, lest we offend them, go to the sea, cast in a hook, and take the fish that comes up first. And when you have opened its mouth, you will find a piece of money; take that and give it to them for Me and you."

The narrative of Elisha and the widow's jar of oil (2 Kings 4:1–7): A certain woman of the wives of the sons of the prophets, came to Elisha and said, "Your servant my husband is dead and you know your servant feared the Lord and the creditor is coming to take my two sons to be his slaves. So, Elisha said to her, "What shall I do for you? Tell me, what do you have in the house?" And she said' "…nothing but a jar of oil…" Elisha then instructed her to borrow vessels from everywhere, go home, shut the door behind her and her sons then pour the oil till the last vessel. She was then instructed to sell the oil, pay the debt, and live on the rest. God provided more than enough for the widow to pay off the debtor and feed her family.

Above all, there are countless situations where God proved himself as a provider, protector, healer, and confidant. The different scenarios and methods he used to meet the needs of the people in desperate circumstances should dispel the fear regarding what will we eat, drink or wear. Our Father in heaven knows and will miraculously provide from his vast resources and the world will marvel.

The time has come for us to shift our focus from the gospel of prosperity, do away with traditions and rituals, and realign ourselves to the gospel of the kingdom of heaven, accept the terms of the great exchange; whereby the king meets the needs of his sons with resources from the home country and in ways that blow away the minds of those who seek to silence the kingdom message from being preached and received.

Chapter 32

Kingdom Currency

Money is the currency of the world. With it you can buy anything on the market, with it you can put a smile on every face. It answers to everything (Ecclesiastes 10:19). Even though money answers to all things on the earth, it answers to nothing in heaven. The currency of the kingdom of heaven is not the dollar, pound, shilling, euro, yen, ruble, cedi, yuan, naira, eco, rupee, franc or rand but Love.

Love is the glue between creation and the Creator. It is not a feeling, neither can it be quantified. Love is life. The value of love radiates from eternity and is not determined by you and me, nor is it affected by socioeconomic factors. Love is universal, it is the currency of the kingdom of heaven.

Love existed before creation and holds the fabric of living and non-living things, including the family and society. No one by themselves can successfully define love unless they know God, who is love (1 John 4:16).

Love is the reason for creation. It was first manifested in heaven when God decided to create mankind in his image and likeness. God was all-in-one and wanted a family to share his love. He had created all the heavenly beings including the angels but there was none in his likeness. He then created man from his being, formed a physical body for him, and gave him a will. Thereafter, he set the male man free that in his freedom, he would choose to love him. (Genesis 1:26; 2:7; Romans 8:38–39). Even as the saying goes, love and compulsion cannot coexist.

After God had made the male man, he saw that there was none among all creation to share the love he had infused inside of him. Man—Adam was all-in-one, and this did not please the Creator. So, he made the female man, whom Adam later called Eve to share the love in Adam. And the amazing love story of Adam and Eve blossomed when he said, "This is now bone of my bones and flesh of my flesh; She shall be called Woman, because she was taken out of Man" (Genesis 2:23). Adam saw another being like himself, but this model was different. It had a womb, hence the name woman. This being with a womb had the capacity to carry and incubate the seed of love—a fetus, that is why she is also called a female. With God, the man and woman, the divine collaboration or triangle to produce the next generation was perfected in love.

This 'love triangle' was short-lived when Adam and Eve disobeyed their Creator and were driven from his presence. However, God is love and love gives regardless of the circumstances. So, his contingency plan was set in motion to restore the broken relationship. God made tunics of skin and clothed them, a foreshadow of the Lamb that would take away the sin of the world (Genesis 3: 21). This is reflected beautifully in the gospel of John that reads, "Behold! The Lamb of God who takes away the sin of the world! (John 1:29). And, "For God so loved the world that He gave His only begotten Son, that whosoever believes in Him should not perish but have eternal life" (John 3:16).

This proves that God is a loving king and, in his kingdom, giving is a key principle of love. It is often quoted, "You can give without loving but you cannot love without giving."[63] God's love for mankind motivated him to extend his kingdom from the invisible to a visible realm for mankind to enjoy dominion, rulership, creativity, stewardship and productivity. In God's kingdom, humans are kings just like their father in heaven, because of the binding tie which is love. The 'constitution' says, "He who does not love does not know God, because God is love" (1 John 4:8).

Love is the missing ingredient on planet earth today because we continue to fabricate and pursue illegitimate sources of love even after we were restored to our source of love—God's presence. Paul described the essence and relevance of love in his letter to the church in Corinth: "Though I speak with the tongues of men and of angels, but have not love, I have become sounding brass or a clanging cymbal. And though I have the gift of prophecy, and understand all mysteries and all knowledge, and though I have all faith, so that I could remove mountains, but have not love, I am nothing. And though I bestow all my goods to feed the poor, and though I give my body to be burned, but have not love, it profits me nothing. Love suffers long and is kind; love does not envy; love does not parade itself, is not puffed up; does not behave rudely, does not seek its own, is not provoked, thinks no evil; does not rejoice in iniquity, but rejoices in the truth; bears all things, believes all things, hopes all things, endures all things. Love never fails" (1 Corinthians 13:1–8).

Now we have the understanding that love never fails and is greater than faith and hope (1 Corinthians 13:8, 13). It is universal and cherished by everyone regardless of race, color, gender, creed, and status. Martin Luther King Jr.'s dream was indeed a passionate call to love; he said, "I have a dream that my four children will one day live in a nation where they will not be judged by the color of their skin, but by the content of their character"[64]. We should judge with love, because when we judge with it, it convicts rather than condemns (John 7:24).

Love is God's character and the greatest gift of God to man. Jesus summarized the law and the prophets into two commandments and said both hang on love. "You shall love your God with all your heart, with all your soul and with all your mind. This is the first and the greatest commandment. And the second is like it: You shall love your neighbor as yourself" (Matthew 22:37–40). When Jesus perceived that the Pharisees and Sadducees were misinterpreting what God had communicated in the Old Testament, regarding loving your neighbor as yourself, he brought the spirit of the law into the interpretation and said, "A new commandment I give to you, that you love one another; as I have loved you" (John 13:34). It is vertical love—God's love, which gives virtue to horizontal love—the love for your neighbor.

If anyone claims to love you but does not love God, run! Forget the so-called songs of love, love seminars and the various human definitions of love. Stop! think before diving into any commitment. Always take God's definition of love into account. Ask yourself, who defines the boundaries and the foundation of that love they seek to share. Always remember anything done out of God's love, will "smell." It is just a matter of time! Therefore, use God's standards to gauge any love offer.

The theme of the greatest love story is, "God is love and mankind the product of it":

> God is love and manifested his love by creating man in his image and likeness. Love is the reason why we exist as God's royal family.
> He loved us so much that he created the physical realm for us to exercise dominion.
> He loved the world so much that he gave his only begotten son to redeem it, so we would have legitimate systems that work for us and not against us.
> God's love never fails!

With such love, why do many still rebel? Deep down in the heart of every human is the love of God. The challenge is that many do not know him, and he only reveals himself to those who genuinely seek to know him. God rules in heaven and operates in the world by love. He loves everyone and every-thing he created. God loves sinners but hates sin, loves liars and thieves but hates lying and stealing, loves fornicators and adulterers but hates fornication and adultery, loves idol worshipers but hates idols and idol worshiping, loves homosexuals but hates homosexuality. God's love for us and the ultimate sacrifice of Jesus, are the remedy for the root cause of sin in our lives (Titus 2:14). But this love has to be accepted.

God's love for humanity regardless of the nature of sin was demonstrated by Jesus when the woman caught in the very act of adultery was brought before him to be stoned to death. He convicted her of sin but did not condemn her to death as the Pharisees had anticipated him to do. Jesus never asked about her sexual history and family background, neither did he ask about her partner in crime, nor did he cast out demons out of her to make a public spectacle as some televangelists and 'men of God' do to attract those seeking miracles and control fol-lowers. God's love convicts unto righteousness (Matthew 16:4; John 16:8). Jesus looked beyond the woman's sin and saw the image and likeness of God in her. Jesus knew his purpose was to seek for the lost and die for their sins. He took the woman's sin upon himself and said from now henceforth, "Go and sin no more" (John 8:1–11). In like manner, Jesus took all our sins upon himself and instructed us to love everyone as he loved us that they may see our good works and believe also (John 15:12; Matthew 5:16). We are admonished to love and be com-passionate unlike the unforgiving debtor who was forgiven so much but could not extend the same measure of patience and understanding to his fellow servant (Matthew 18:21–35).

True love originates from the heart of God who is love. Love obeys and protects. You cannot say you love God and disobey his word, neither can you say you love him and pervert sexuality, lie, steal and curse. Any type of love, be it unconditional (*agape*), romantic (*eros*), affectionate (*philia*), self-love (*philautia*), familial (*storge*), enduring (*pragma*), playful (*ludus*) and obsessive (*mania*) should take its roots from God.[65] After all God is the ultimate lover and source of all love. It is he who gave us self-identity, created family units, established social constructs, and built in us sexual feelings and set the boundaries of sexual expressions and fulfillment within the confines of divine love in holy matrimony. God cannot ask you to do anything he has not equipped you for. If we surrender to him our desires, be there greed, lust, anger, unforgiveness and any form of ungodliness, he will turn our hearts and fill us with godly desires, love, peace, and divine thoughts.

As we love God and one another, even as Jesus loved us and gave himself for us, we become partners or co-workers with God in the rebuilding of the kingdom of heaven on earth. Kingdom living on earth is how we display the love for our home country, because every citizen treasures his home country and seeks to contribute to its advancement. This is explained by Jesus in scriptures when he said that, wherever a man's heart is there his treasures would be and cautioned us to store up treasures in the dominion mandate to make the earth look just like heaven.

Anyone who loves Jesus should speak and preach the truth in love for everyone to gladly receive the grace package made available over two thousand years ago. We are not to focus on people's shortcomings, religions, or rituals, rather show them the love and grace of God that comes by faith in Jesus Christ. We are to love everyone and lead a life that exemplifies Jesus (John 13:35). As believers we are expected to prop and support the wounded and not 'throw them away', because even though they may stumble and fall they remain the righteousness of God (Philemon 1:8–15). One cannot leave to see change in a person who they cast away or killed, so let us emulate Jesus and others who have walked in his footsteps because

> ➢ Jesus forgave and prayed for those who crucified him, and they became witnesses to his resurrection power (Luke 23:34; Matthew 27:54).
> ➢ Jesus never called down fire to consume Peter when he tried to persuade him against God's will. Jesus instead turned and rebuked the spirit behind what Peter said and not Peter the person (Matthew 16:22–23).
> ➢ Jesus rebuked Peter and James for making the request to call down fire from heaven to consume the people of Samaria when they rejected him (Luke 9:54–56).
> ➢ Stephen the martyr forgave his murderers and Saul at whose feet the witnesses laid down their clothes. Saul went on to become Paul the apostle after he was knocked off his horse by the same Jesus that Stephen had confessed during his martyrdom (Acts 7:54–60, 9:3–5).

> ➢ Jesus did not create any form of classism between him-
>   self and others but blended in so much they had to pay
>   someone to single him out (Luke 22:47–48).

After the cross, God does not judge us based on our past but on
our belief in Christ Jesus. Our behavior or choices determine
how we enjoy our rights and privileges while on earth. Behavior change is, therefore, a divine inclination for all believers who conform to the Word of God by the renewal of their
minds. A renewed mind is the key to manifesting our heavenly
citizenship on planet earth.

To show that we love God is to obey his commands. Anything done in the name of the Lord, without love is sin. True
love understands and values things. When we love God,
we value the expansion of his kingdom on the earth. God
is a giver and loves a cheerful giver, not a tearful one. Giving cheerfully is the new covenant principle (2 Corinthians
9:7-8). In the old covenant, one had to give in tears to be
blessed (Psalm 126: 5). They had to perform to be blessed—a
performance-based relationship, which the Bible calls dead
works and self-righteousness. In the new dispensation, we
are already blessed and have a sonship inheritance-based relationship with God.

As sons of the kingdom, we have covenant rights and privileges to all kingdom resources. However, when these are not
manifesting in our lives, we should ask God to reveal what is
hindering us from receiving and enjoying his unlimited resources. Questions to consider include: Are our desires in line

with God's will? Are we good stewards and have work plans for our lives? Do we have some skeletons in our closet? Do we take full responsibility for our decisions and shortcomings? Is our love genuine and built on a strong foundation? As sons in this dispensation, obedience allows us to fully enjoy our rights and privileges.

We are to be excellent ambassadors, who love and lay up treasures in the home country by applying the king's government policies and programs to the resident country. This is not about sending wealth back home but utilizing and investing the resources given by the home government to impact and change the resident country to look just like home.

Love is the umbilical cord between the home country and the resident country. Love is the reason for this book—love for our king, his kingdom, his royal family, and the world. It may not be perfect but serves as a beacon for us to re-examine our laws and policies, our beliefs, faith, and religions. Everyone's right and opinion regarding knowledge and divine revelation, are respected but as fellows in one ship with God, we should be committed to serving, helping, loving and supporting one another to fulfill the assignment of extending the governing influence of the kingdom of heaven throughout the earth.

Endnotes

1. Myles Munroe, Kingdom Principles (2006)

2. Frazier H.C., *In Shakespeare and Dying Declarations (1985)*

3. Urban Dictionary.com, *Come-to-Jesus-moment* (2020)

4. Frances J. Crosby, *Blessed Assurance* (1873)

5. John Newton, *Amazing Grace* (1779)

6. Joseph P. Webster, *The Sweet By-and-By* (1968)

7. Abraham Lincoln, *Proclamation Appointing National Fast Day*, Washington, D.C (March, 1863)

8. Ev. Immortel Kaniki Official, *youtube.com/watch?v=30vD6KH-Rto* (June 25,2019)

9. See John 1:1-3; Proverbs 33:6-9; Psalm 136:5; Genesis 1; Hebrews 1:1-5; 11:3)

10. Houghton Mifflin Harcourt publishing company, *The American Heritage® Dictionary of the English Language* (Fifth Edition copyright ©2020)

11. Albert Einstein, *We cannot solve our problems with the same thinking we used when we created them* (n.d.)

12. See Matthew 16:18-19

13. The Editors of Encyclopedia Britannica, *Ecclesia of ancient Greek assembly* (1768)

14. Jessica Taylor, *Trump To Values Voters: In America 'We Don't Worship Government, We Worship God* (npr.org 2017)

15. Frederick Lewis Donaldson, *Seven Social Sins* (West-minster Abbey 1925)

16. Albert E. Brumley, *I'll Fly Away* (1932)

17. Johnny Cash, *I Got Shoes* (1962)

18. See, Matthew 6:33; Revelation 12:12; John 17:16; Ephesians 2:6; Romans 16:20.

19. Don Moen, *God Will Make a Way* (1992)

20. Fanny Crosby, *Pass Me Not O Gentle Savior* (1868)

21. Myles Munroe, *Rediscovering the Kingdom: Ancient Hope of Our 21st Century World* (Shippensburg, PA: Destiny Image Publishers, 2004)

22. Ucg.org, *Did Roman Gods morph into Christian Saints?* (2007)

23. George Orwell, *A people that elect corrupt politicians* (1940s)

24. David Maraga, *A year largely defined by politics* (nation. co.ke 2017)

25. Saint Augustine, *Without God man cannot, and without man, God will not, quote* (5th Century)

26. Henri Nouwen, *In the Name of Jesus*, 57–60 (1990s)

27. Robert Ingersoll, *Said About Lincoln* (1883)

28. Mahatma Gandhi, *The day the power of love overrules the love of power, the world will know peace, Quotable Quote*

29. Robert Greene, *The 48 Laws of Power* (1998)

30. Dorian Lynskey, *The Guardian Robert Greene on his 48 Laws of Power* (2012)

31. Karl Mark, *A Contribution to the Critique of Hegel's Philosophy of Right,* (1843)

32. Desmond Tutu, *In Paul Vallery: Missionary must stop preaching* (2001)

33. Sir Francis Bacon, *Meditationes Sacrae and Human Philosophy* (1597)

34. Thomas Jefferson, *Separation between Church & State* (1802)

35. Constitution Annotated, *Analysis and interpretation of the U.S Constitution,* constitution.congress.gov/browse/amendment-1/

36. President Dwight D. Eisenhower signs a law officially declaring *"In God We Trust" to be the nation's official motto, (This Day in History 30 July 1956)*

37. Franco Ordonez, *Trump Defends School Prayer* (npr. org 2020)

38. Steven Runciman, *A history of Crusades* (1951)

39. Blaise Pascal, *Pensées* (1623–1662)

40. Mother Miriam, *Popes Proposal for 'new humanism' would wipe out Christianity* (lifesiteNews 2019)

41. Hill K.A., *The Winners' Guide* (2015)

42. Donald R. McClarey: the-american-catholic.com, *PopeWatch*: New Humanism (2019)

43. Irina Bokova, *A new Humanism for the 21st Century* (2010)

44. Carl Coon, *Progressive Humanism* (1998)

45. Corliss Lamont, *The Philosophy of Humanism* (New York: Frederick Unger Publishing Company, 1965)

46. Pete Baklinski, *LifeSiteNews* (2020)

47. Jules Gomes, *ChurchMilitant.com* (2020)

48. Tim Challies, *In the Incomparable Christ* (2015)

49. Brothers Emmanuel & Lazarus, Voice of the Cross in *What manner of man is Jesus?* Christian/Gospel (2015)

50. Rachel Zoll, *The Associated Press* (2010)

51. Sarah Jakes Roberts, *Lost and Found: Finding Hope in the Detours of Life* (2014)

52. Benjamin Franklin, *In his Poor Richard's Almanack* (1736)

53. Doris Curtis and Bryan Curtis, *Inspirational Thoughts to warm the Soul* (2011)

54. Daniel Silliman, *Benny Hinn Renounces His Selling of God's Blessings* (2019)

55. Jesusonline.com, *Another Prosperity Preacher Joyce Meyer Denounces Prosperity Gospel, Premiered* (2019)

56. see Matthew 24; 1 Thessalonians 4:16-17; 2 Thessalonians 2:3-7

57. see Daniel 2:44-45; Isaiah 9:6-7; Revelation 5:9-10; 20:1-3, 10; 21:1-4

58. tommorowsworld.org/magazines/2018/July-August/thecoming-one-world-government

59. see Galatians 6:17; Luke 17:21; Ephesians 1:13; Revelation 13:16-18; 19:20

60. The Politics of a COVID-19 Vaccine: www.cfr.org/article/politics-covid-19-vaccine

61. The Great Reset: A Unique Twin Summit to Begin 2021, weforum.org

62. Donald R. McClarey: the-american-catholic.com, *PopeWatch*: New Humanism (2019)

63. Amy Wilson Carmichael, *In His Hands* (1867–1951)

64. Martin Luther King Jr. "I HAVE A DREAM..." On August 28 in 1963, Reported in the Nobel Peace Prize (1964)

65. Jack Zavada, *Learnreligions.com/types-of-love-in-the-bible-700177* (2020)

CPSIA information can be obtained
at www.ICGtesting.com
Printed in the USA
LVHW050719181020
668893LV00002B/140